S0-CQS-756

11/24
STRAND PRICE
$5.00

LOST PAGES
FROM
AMERICAN HISTORY

LOST PAGES FROM AMERICAN HISTORY

Webb Garrison

Stackpole Books

LOST PAGES FROM AMERICAN HISTORY

Copyright © 1976 by
Webb Garrison

Published by
STACKPOLE BOOKS
Cameron and Kelker Streets
Harrisburg, Pa. 17105

All rights reserved, including the right to reproduce this book or portions thereof in any form or by any means, electronic or mechanical, including photocopying, recording, or by any information storage and retrieval system, without permission in writing from the publisher. All inquiries should be addressed to Stackpole Books, Cameron and Kelker Streets, Harrisburg, Pennsylvania 17105.

Printed in the U.S.A.

Library of Congress Cataloging in Publication Data

Garrison, Webb B
    Lost pages from American history.

    1. United States   History—Miscellanea.
I. Title.
E179.G26   973'.08   75-34351
ISBN 0-8117-0959-0

Contents

Introduction

Every attempt to interpret men and events involves a process of winnowing and sifting. In order to describe some things others must be ignored, or relegated to footnotes. As a result, much of the drama plus some of the bone and sinew of the past is lost from the pages of every conventional volume of history.

Addressed to the general reader, this volume represents an attempt to restore balance. It comes to focus upon persons and events seldom if ever treated in textbooks. Yet it deals with processes and persons significant to the American drama.

Much of the research has, necessarily, been concentrated upon sources not generally accessible. Newspapers, magazines, and private papers have made important contributions. Numerous historical societies plus state and local libraries have given cheerful and generous cooperation.

Prepared with great care but frequently surprising and hopefully often entertaining, this volume is designed as a "fun book" that will also serve as a reference tool.

Grateful acknowledgment is made for encouragement received from publishers of newspapers in whose pages some portions of many vignettes were treated in different style: The *National Enquirer;* The Indianapolis *News;* and the Evansville, Indiana, *Press*.

WEBB GARRISON

9

"Washington City" remained a sleepy river village long after it was designated as the new site of the U.S. government

Political "Log Rolling" Placed the Permanent Capital of the U.S. on Then-Desolate Banks of the Potomac River

Noted French designer and builder Pierre Charles L'Enfant won lasting fame as the architect who laid out Washington, D.C. But it was the doggedness and political acumen of one American—Alexander Hamilton—that led to the selection of the site on which L'Enfant planned "the ideal city."

Movements of British troops plus sectional rivalry had caused the Continental Congress to shift the site of its sessions from one place to another. First Philadelphia, then Baltimore. Back to Philadelphia and

11

on to York and to Lancaster, Pennsylvania, before returning to Philadelphia. On to Princeton, Annapolis, Trenton and finally, New York City.

Changes in the seat of government made it awkward and sometimes impossible for legislators to take along records and files. Travel was often so difficult that attendance was low; meeting in Nassau Hall (a college building) at Princeton, business was conducted by just twenty-two members. Long before independence became assured, there was an attempt to establish a permanent seat of government. The November, 1779, suggestion that first entered official records favored purchase of "a few square miles near Princeton village, whereon to erect public offices and buildings."

If city fathers of Kingston, New York, knew of the sentiment favoring Princeton, they looked at it askance. Early in 1783 they asked the state legislature to put its weight behind their proposal to grant Congress one square mile within the limits of the town of Kingston as "a separate district for the Honorable Congress of the United States." Alexander Hamilton, who later became the most influential figure in the fight for location of the capital, persuaded New Yorkers to increase the Kingston offer to two square miles.

Nothing came of the proposal, though. Neither was there any action upon an offer from Annapolis in May of the same year. In June, New Jersey offered to provide a site anywhere in the colony. Virginia countered by proposing to give up the town of Williamsburg plus 300 acres of land and cash not exceeding £100,000.

Then meeting in Philadelphia, Congress proposed to take up the various offers in October. Long before that date rolled around, mutinous unpaid Revolutionary soldiers forced lawmakers to flee from Independence Hall. They adjourned hastily with plans to meet eight days later in Princeton; some vowed never again to convene in the City of Brotherly Love. A committee headed by James Madison solemnly considered the matter of a permanent seat of government and submitted a formal report on September 18, 1783.

No action was taken by Congress, but one aspect of the Madison report quickly gained informal but lasting concensus. The permanent site of national government would be a "federal district" under direct control of Congress and not included in the boundaries of any state. Such a concept, which required a radical break with European tradition, was not absolutely novel. Centuries earlier, aware of intense

"Washington City" as it appeared in 1800
—Library of Congress

rivalry between Israel and Judah, King David had established Jerusalem as just such a federal capital.

It would take more than the wisdom of David, though, to persuade rival delegations to yield their claims for the prize. Briefly, lawmakers seriously considered having not one but two capitals. Francis Hopkinson ridiculed that proposal by suggesting that a recently-authorized statue of George Washington should be "placed on wheels and be taken to the site of the nation's business, wherever that might be."

Adoption of the Constitution in 1787 settled for all time the question of jurisdiction—which was given to Congress in keeping with prevailing sentiment. But the matter of location remained a wide-open and hotly-debated issue. New York, the site of government at the time our first president was inaugurated, naturally wanted to remain the political as well as financial center of the nation. A southern bloc led by James Madison and Richard Lee argued persuasively for a capital on the banks of the Potomac River—"geographically, the center of the United States."

George Washington made no secret of the fact that he'd like very much to see the government centered near his beloved Mount Vernon.

But even his enormous prestige was not enough to sway northern votes. Lawmakers were in a hopeless deadlock with the line of division being geographical: north versus south.

Congress had shown itself impotent to act upon another issue that many considered far more pressing. Debts incurred by the several colonies that later became independent states were staggering. Secretary of the Treasury Alexander Hamilton had drafted and presented an Assumption Bill under which the new nation would assume the debts of its member states. No other course seemed remotely likely to restore credit and bring economic stability. But war debts of northern states were generally much greater than those of southern. Many southern delegates balked at helping to foot bills run up by northerners. Hamilton was a few votes short of having the number required to pass his Assumption Bill—and there was no indication that its foes would yield.

In this critical situation, Thomas Jefferson returned from France to become Washington's Secretary of State. According to Jefferson's own decidedly lame explanations years afterward, his four-year absence made him ignorant of internal dissension so great that some members of Congress were beginning to talk of withdrawing from the new union.

Hamilton was a veteran practitioner of the subtle art of political vote-trading, or "log rolling." He saw his opportunity and rose to the occasion superbly. In a private meeting with Jefferson, he proposed that if the Secretary of State would persuade a few southerners to vote for the Assumption Bill, the Secretary of the Treasury—properly grateful—would persuade a few northerners to throw their weight behind the proposal to locate the permanent capital of the U.S. in the south.

Precisely how many votes were traded is a matter of conjecture; clearly, it was not more than a handful. But a switch of one or two senators and perhaps half a dozen representatives was enough. Congress voted to have the U.S. assume war debts of the states—and to locate the federal capital on the banks of the Potomac (where George Washington wanted it).

A July 16, 1790, bill established Philadelphia as the site of Congress until the first Monday in December, 1800. Then the government would move to a Potomac River site. George Washington himself negotiated terms under which on March 30, 1791, nineteen landed proprietors ceded their rights—some reluctantly—to about 600 acres needed to supplement land given by Virginia.

Even when the official transfer of power from Philadelphia to the new federal city was made in 1800, Washington was "a mud hole in the middle of a forest." Congressman John C. Smith of Connecticut described Pennsylvania Avenue as "a deep morass covered with elder bushes." Northern newspapers dubbed it "the Serbonian Bog." Portugal's minister to the U.S., the witty Abbe Correa de Serra, took a look at the new capital and dubbed it "the city of magnificent distances."

Senator Gouverneur Morris, in a private letter, confessed that "We only need here houses, cellars, kitchens, scholarly men, amiable women, and a few other such trifles to possess a perfect city, for we can walk over it as we would in the fields and woods, and, on account of a strong frost, the air is quite pure." Abigail Adams, on her way to the new "presidential palace" that was far from finished, lost her way in the woods and with her party wandered for two hours before being rescued.

From the steps of the Capitol, according to contemporary accounts, a person could count "seven or eight boarding-houses, one tailor's shop, one shoemaker's, one printing establishment, the home of a washwoman, a dry-goods house and an oyster market." It was from that beginning—determined not by national sentiment but by political vote-trading—that present-day Washington, D.C., rose from the wilderness.

Governor William Franklin, staunchly Tory son of Benjamin

Benjamin Franklin's Son, Disowned after a Quarrel over Politics, Never Effected a Reconciliation with His Father

William Franklin (1731-1813) was the last British governor of New Jersey. He was the "natural" (illegitimate) son of Benjamin Franklin and until middle life was the apple of his father's eye. During the American Revolution, William turned against democracy and his father. He remained a staunch Tory so was disowned by Benjamin; later attempts at reconciliation were unsuccessful.

Much evidence supports the view that William was the son of Benjamin's common-law wife, Deborah Read. But there is no documentary evidence. Though most Americans vaguely remember that

Ben Franklin's son was involved in his famous kite experiment, few pause to wonder how he got there—or what became of him. Silence of history books may be due to respect for the memory of one of America's most gifted leaders.

Benjamin Franklin's son grew up in Philadelphia, where he showed "great fondness for books." Later he entered military service and acquitted himself so well that he became a captain in the Pennsylvania forces at eighteen. A year later his famous father wrote of him: "William is now nineteen years of age, a tall proper Youth, and much of a Beau. He acquired a habit of idleness in the military expedition, but begins of late to apply himself to business. I hope he will become an industrious man."

It was Billy who got his father's kite into the air in 1752 when the latter showed electricity to be "the vital force in lightning." But instead of the boy of twelve or fifteen who is universally depicted in that incident, Billy was actually a military veteran aged twenty-one. For his role in the investigation of lightning, Billy won the M.A. degree from Oxford University.

Benjamin Franklin started writing his famous *Autobiography* for his son—partly because of gratitude for Billy's role in helping to draw electricity from the sky.

Through his father's influence young William served for a period as clerk of the house of the Assembly of Pennsylvania. Then Benjamin got him an appointment as comptroller of the general postoffice—a job he held from 1754 to 1756. When his father went to England in 1756 as agent for Pennsylvania, William resigned from his post and went with him.

In England young Franklin studied law and was admitted to the bar. William Strahan, a close friend of his father, described William as "one of the prettiest young gentlemen I ever knew from America. His father is at one and the same time his friend, his brother, his intimate and easy companion."

Both of the Franklins became close friends of Scottish-born John Stuart, Earl of Bute. Bute was a lord of the bedchamber to the Prince of Wales, so had great influence when the prince became King George III in 1760. Almost as soon as George III ascended the throne he began getting recommendations from Bute that William Franklin be appointed to a high post in the colonies.

After secret negotiations, in August, 1762, the monarch named

Benjamin Franklin's son as royal governor of New Jersey. "Know you that we reposing especial trust and confidence in the prudence courage and loyalty of you, the said William Franklin, have thought fit to constitute and appoint you to be our Captain General and Governor in Chief in and over our provinces of Nova Caesarea or New Jersey," the royal commission read in part.

With his father as an onlooker, William placed his hand upon a Bible and swore to obey and uphold the authority of King George III in New Jersey. Governor Franklin reached that colony from England on February 23, 1763. He was well received and showed himself to be an able administrator.

But tensions that had been mounting between Britain and her American colonies for a decade reached a crisis point in 1774. On February 2 of that year the elder Franklin wrote his son to urge: "I wish you were well settled on your farm. 'Tis an honester and a more honourable because a more independent employment."

Later that year, father and son met at Perth Amboy and had a long talk about the conflict that both saw as inevitable. Benjamin urged American resistance at any cost; his son disagreed and insisted that his loyalties were totally committed to the English crown.

Benjamin Franklin sadly chose to put loyalty to his country above love for his son. Brief notes that he made when the First Continental Congress assembled indicate that he recognized himself to be "perhaps the loneliest man in the crowded chamber of the Pennsylvania State House." That loneliness stemmed from the fact that at a distance of only half a day's journey, Governor Franklin was persuading members of the New Jersey Assembly to "avoid exposing this fair land to the royal heel."

The break between father and son was complete. Benjamin was wholly committed to armed rebellion; William was equally dedicated to England and the king. So Governor Franklin remained at his post after armed conflict broke out, and continued to collect and transmit intelligence to England.

On June 15, 1776, the Provincial Congress of New Jersey declared Benjamin Franklin's son to be "an enemy to the liberties of this country," and ordered his arrest. He was sent as a prisoner to Connecticut, and for a time was quartered at East Windsor. In 1778 he was exchanged and released, so went to New York for a four-year stay during which he served for a time as President of the Board of Associated Loyalists (or Tories).

Benjamin Franklin with grandsons on streets of Paris (from watercolor by Henry A Ogden)

The son of America's great diplomat, scientist, and philosopher left his homeland in 1782 and never came back. As compensation for the losses he had sustained the English government granted him a cash settlement of £1,800 plus a pension of £800 per year for life.

Ten years after he had quarreled with his father over politics William tried to effect a reconciliation. His letter of August, 1784, addressed the elder Franklin as "Dear and honoured father," and begged that they might "revive that affectionate intercourse and connexion which till the commencement of the late troubles had been the pride and happiness of my life."

Benjamin Franklin's reply stressed that "Indeed nothing has ever hurt me so much and affected me with such keen sensations, as to find myself deserted in my old age by my only son; and not only deserted, but to find him taking up arms against me, in a cause, wherein my good fame, fortune, and life were all at stake."

The two men met, briefly and awkwardly, several times in Paris. They talked stiffly but made little progress. Benjamin Franklin liked to stroll along the boulevards with his grandsons, but refused to be seen in public with William.

On January 1, 1788, Benjamin Franklin referred to the matter in a letter he wrote to the Rev. Dr. Byles of Boston. "My son is estranged from me by the part he took in the late war, and keeps aloof," he said. "The part he acted against me, which is of public notoriety, will account for my leaving him no more of an estate he endeavoured to deprive me of."

The estate to which Franklin referred was very large by today's standards. But at the death of the Sage of Philadelphia, his only son was left nothing but a barren tract of land in Nova Scotia plus "the books and papers in his possession." Embittered by his self-chosen exile, William Franklin died in England on November 17, 1813.

Though specialists in colonial history were aware of the bitter quarrel between father and son, the extent of Benjamin Franklin's emotional involvement was not discovered until recent times. In 1964 the Franklin Institute made public a long-lost will drawn up in 1757 when the Sage of Philadelphia was in New York waiting for passage to England. He prepared the document because of danger of attack at sea.

Income from Franklin's printing business, which yielded profits equivalent to more than $50,000 a year by modern standards, were in 1757 divided equally between Deborah Read, William Franklin, and Benjamin's daughter Sarah. But during the very period in which William was seeking reconciliation, his famous father drew up a new will leaving his son only a token inheritance.

General Jubal Early, Confederate States of America

While Jubal Early's Confederates Paused to Collect Ransom, Union Forces Strengthened the Defense of Washington

Carved out of semi-wilderness in order to become the site of a federal capital, the District of Columbia at first had a powerful geographical appeal. Even those delegates who wanted to establish the center of government in New York or Philadelphia conceded that the site favored by George Washington and destined to bear his name was about as close to the center of the new nation as one could hope it to be. Sixty years of westward expansion left the once-central capital dangling in the easternmost strip of the nation. Then secession drew east-west lines of such nature that Washington—dangerously close to Confederate soil—was too rich a prize for rebels to ignore.

Confederate General Jubal ("Jubilee") Early moved into the Shenandoah Valley in the spring of 1864 with the overt goal of stopping Union forces led by David F. Hunter. At Staunton, Virginia, men in blue who were commanded by Crook and Averell joined Hunter in order to form what seemed a nearly-invincible force of 18,000 seasoned men who sang of victory as they marched south.

Jubilee Early, with 30,000 men, moved out from Cold Harbor in time to be in position as Hunter's forces approached Lynchburg. Recognizing himself to be out-maneurvered and out-manned, the Union leader turned and retreated instead of making a full-scale attack. Later, Hunter lamely excused decisions that led to one of the most dramatic periods of the Civil War as having been occasioned by his lack of adequate ammunition.

He had enough firepower to pepper advancing Confederates and engage in frequent skirmishes. Still, Hunter led his men all the way through the long valley into the edge of West Virginia—with gray-clad troops close on his heels. The maneuver that Hunter described as "a strategic withdrawal" left Confederates clearly in command of the Shenandoah Valley—where any amateur could see that Washington was likely to become a target.

In spite of frantic telegrams from the capital, most troops racing to its defense were still days away. By Friday, July 8, only a motley group of raw short-term men under the command of General Lew Wallace stood between Early and the nerve center of the Union. On July 9th Early's men fought valiantly along the Monocacy River, thirty miles from Washington, but suffered 2000 casualties to 700 Confederate losses. The engagement ended not in a defeat, but in a rout.

According to contemporary accounts, "Terror gripped Washington City." Arms were issued to civilian employees of governmental agencies and rude fortifications were thrown up by untrained men. According to the *Independent Line*, "clerks of the Adjutant General's office were drilling in front of Lafayette Square, fully armed and equipped." Except for Major General Horatio Wright's VI Corps, there was no strong body of seasoned Union troops within the nation's capital.

Speculation—and rumor—abounded. Newspapers incorrectly estimated the strength of Early's forces at 45,000 veterans. Perhaps he would strike quickly in order to loot the federal treasury . . . or even to take Abraham Lincoln prisoner, and then withdraw. Or he might burn

Visiting McClellan's troops in Frederick, Md., Abraham Lincoln told cheering crowds that he hoped "Americans for a thousand generations will enjoy the blessings of a united nation."

and loot in the capital before pressing into southern Maryland to free 17,000 Confederates imprisoned at Point Lookout. Rumor, later verified, had it that through Horace Greeley, Lincoln had invited any citizen to step forward if he had a peace proposal whose only conditions would be restoration of the Union and abolition of slavery.

No one knows who spawned the idea that proved to keep rebel forces from penetrating Washington past the 7th Street line (well inside the District of Columbia). But someone—perhaps Early himself or one of his top aides—conceived the idea of "levying a contribution" instead of burning a captured Union city. Early's subordinate, John McCausland, demanded—and got—$20,000 on July 6 in return for sparing Hagerstown, Maryland, from the torch.

Defeat of Lew Wallace at the Monocacy River left a much finer plum in Confederate hands. Frederick, Maryland, with a population of about 8000, was a city by standards of the era. Many fine old buildings lined its streets; families who had gained their wealth from plantations and from commercial enterprises lived in mansions that helped to give Frederick its air of elegance.

Even though the federal dollar had shrunk in purchasing power to about thirty-nine cents, Confederates badly needed dollars for the purchase of war supplies in Europe. Jubilee Early demanded a "contribution" of $200,000 from citizens of Frederick. City fathers indicated eagerness to comply with his terms, but said they'd have to have time—at least twenty-four hours. Early pondered alternatives, decided to wait for the money instead of sacking the city, and duly collected the entire ransom.

While Early waited for his money, invalids and "hundred-day men" (drafted hurriedly for that period) were armed and organized. Federal troops began to reach the threatened city; some came up the Potomac by boat, others overland by forced march. Though many of them had never seen action, an estimated 20,000 soldiers in blue— greatly strengthened by being in a defensive rather than an offensive position—waited for Early and his men.

Confederates invaded the outer edges of Washington on July 11, but never made the major assault that was universally feared. The one-day delay brought about by the wait for Frederick's "contribution" was just enough to alter the balance of power. Confederates made a desultory attack upon Ft. Stevens while Lincoln was there to inspect the fortification. Oliver Wendell Holmes, Jr., twenty-three years old and unaware that he was destined to sit on the Supreme Court for nearly thirty years, shouted to the president: "Get down, you fool!"

That was as close as Jubilee Early came to getting his hands upon the President of the United States. Had he thrown his troops forward at full speed in the aftermath of crushing the forces of Lew Wallace, the history of the U.S. might have been different.

Maryland Senators Charles Mathias and J. Glenn Beall gave such weight to that crucial twenty-four-hour delay in Frederick that in 1970 they tried to get the federal government to reimburse the town that had saved Washington. At four percent interest, the original "contribution" of $200,000 would have swelled to about $6 million—a small price, they argued, for precious hours during which Union forces strengthened the defense of Washington.

Lawmakers from other regions opposed the restitution on the grounds that it would open a "Civil War pandora's box." Defeat of the bill for reimbursement of the city of Frederick relegated its all-important non-military action in the summer of 1864 to a lost page in American history.

John Wise, center of gondola, gestures for ropes to be released for take-off at 6:40 P.M. on July 1, 1859 (St. Louis)

In The Balloon *Atlantic* Astronaut John Wise Set a Distance Record that Stood for 51 Years

In the era before the Civil War self-taught astronaut John Wise, now practically unknown, dreamed of an era when freight and passengers would go back and forth between American and Europe by air. He was so sure that he was right that he named one of his balloons the *Atlantic*. Hoping by means of a spectacular flight in the craft to get Congressional funding for trans-Atlantic attempts, he crashed in a forest near Henderson, New York. But before he landed in a treetop he had established a distance record for travel in the air that was not broken until 1910.

Born and educated in Lancaster, Pennsylvania, Wise (like the

Wright Brothers and other persons famous in aviation) didn't approach the matter of travel through the air by means of science, or even logic. As a boy of fourteen, reading his father's German-language newspaper, he came across an account of a balloon voyage to Italy. It so fired the mind of the adolescent that, on his own, he began to experiment with "aerostatics."

Paper parchutes dropped from three-story buildings stimulated his curiosity instead of satisfying it. Since paper burst easily the boy began experimenting with ox bladders; using four of them, he anticipated the space age by testing his ideas with an animal. Wise chose a cat—which landed unharmed, from a height of thirty feet.

That safe though involuntary journey by a cat turned his interest from a boyhood hobby into a lifelong obsession. As he watched the slow descent of the animal, young Wise was "caught up by yearning to experience the sublime feeling of sailing in the air." That was in 1833, when few Americans knew about exploits of European pioneers and even fewer were interested.

John Wise couldn't become a balloonist without money; in order to get money he had to learn a trade. While working in Philadelphia as apprentice cabinetmaker and later as a maker of pianos, he read every scrap of information he could find about aeronautics and experimented with unmanned craft of his own construction. A few of his balloons ascended 10,000 feet into the air—where their movements showed him what he believed to be a steady and fast wind blowing from west to east.

That west wind, announced youthful John Wise, would take a lighter-than-air craft from the U.S. to Europe in about fifty hours. Most persons ignored such nonsense. A few influential men were sufficiently impressed to put their support behind a movement to persuade Congress to appropriate $15,000 so that the American astronaut could test his theory. Few lawmakers were interested. To get the money, Wise realized, he'd have to "shake the country by its teeth." What better way to do just that than to make a "truly epochal voyage through the air"?

No mere dreamy adventurer, John Wise was intensely practical and though self-taught knew more about the budding science of aeronautics than most men who had received university training. Though hot air had been successfully used by the Montgolfier brothers and other Europeans, he reasoned correctly that fire hazards involved in a long voyage "dictated the choice of other lifting power, necessarily lighter than ordinary air.'' After many tests he settled on highly-inflammable lighting gas then widely made by heating coal. In order to get the congressional appropriation he wanted he'd have to show that aerial transportation could benefit the world of business and finance.

That's why he placed a heavy mailbag in the wicker basket slung under the balloon *Atlantic* when he and three passengers lifted off from St. Louis late on the afternoon of July 1, 1859. Nearly sixty feet high and about fifty feet in diameter, the *Atlantic* glistened from the special varnish that Wise had compounded. Had a veteran French or English astronaut been on hand for the liftoff he would have been puzzled by a feature then unknown in Europe. The *Atlantic* was equipped with another Wise invention —a rip cord that, when pulled, converted the craft into a clumsy but (comparatively) effective parachute for emergency descent. Both rip cord and varnish were destined to become standard features of later balloons.

Once rigging of the *Atlantic* was properly adjusted, the balloon and the gondola suspended by thirty-six heavy ropes ascended gracefully (and by standards of the era extremely swiftly) to the 12,000-foot level. There her navigator found the steady west wind he was seeking, and calculated that speed was approaching sixty miles an hour.

Measured by all indicators, it would have seemed that America had entered the air age—nearly two years before Fort Sumter surrendered to Confederate forces. Passengers carried by the *Atlantic*— including a reporter for the Missouri *Republican* who hoped to scoop every other newsman in the country—became conscious of extreme cold as their initial exhilaration waned. Still they sped along at so even a keel that John Wise sent his three companions into the boat slung beneath the customary wicker basket and stretched out for a nap.

That all-important west wind proved to be considerably more erratic than Wise had expected. Moving northward as well as eastward, the *Atlantic* reached Lake Erie about twelve hours after liftoff. By now the wind was blowing at a rate estimated (incorrectly) to be ninety miles an hour. Much of the balloon's half-ton of sand ballast had already been used; when the craft dipped dangerously close to white caps on the surface of the roaring Lake Ontario, Wise cut loose the boat brought along for use in the event of an emergency landing in water.

By now every man aboard knew that winds were taking them on a zigzag course rather than the due east course they had anticipated. John LaMountain, a former seaman who had helped to build the craft,

While passing over Lake Ontario, the ATLANTIC came perilously close to falling into wind-lashed water

became violently ill under its lurching. Every man aboard breathed a silent prayer of gratitude when land was sighted shortly before 2 p.m. Acting without orders from his chief, LaMountain threw out the grapnel. It caught, but lines snapped instantly and the *Atlantic*—badly out of balance—careened forward wildly until a lull in the wind deposited the already-battered gondola (minus its vital mail pouch) high in the branches of a huge tree. Instead of receiving plaudits from residents of Manhattan, as planned, the astronauts were alone in a forest not far from Henderson, N.Y.

Wise, who may have overestimated deviations from the straight course, calculated that the *Atlantic* had covered more than 1100 miles in nineteen hours. According to the best measurement of the era, the bee-line distance from liftoff to what space-age astronauts term splashdown was 804 miles. Only the slow communications of the era and the gathering clouds that pointed to Civil War prevented the voyage of the *Atlantic* from becoming one of the classic American stories of adventure mingled with science, for the distance record established during that stormy night and day was not surpassed by any "astronaut" in any type of aircraft until 1910.

Wise made more than 400 balloon ascents before he crashed to his death at age seventy-one while testing the *Pathfinder*. He never got so much as a token "research grant" of the type now freely handed out by the federal government. Backed by the New York *Daily Graphic* he planned—but never actually attempted—a balloon flight across the sea whose name was borne by the *Atlantic*. Many later astornauts, well financed and equipped with instruments developed in modern times, have tried and have failed to equal the epochal voyage of that craft. Had Americans not been preoccupied with sectional differences, the *Atlantic* might have had us move toward passenger and mail service by air a full half-century earlier.

William O. Stoddard's 1888 interpretation of "Vice-president Tyler Receiving the News of President Harrison's Death" —a widely circulated but highly improbable view
(wood engraving; Library of Congress)

In the Midst of Bitter Infighting among Whigs, Skinny John Tyler Literally Seized—and Kept—The White House

On September 17, 1787, thrity-nine delegates to the federal convention in Philadelphia approved and signed the United States Constitution. William Gladstone later called it "the most wonderful work ever struck off at a given time by the brain and purpose of man." But however able and dedicated the delegates were, many of them were bone-weary and eager to get a job done. Some later commentators upon their work have called it "a bundle of compromises and a mosaic of second choices."

If that verdict is too harsh, it is beyond dispute that framers of the Constitution failed in some instances to state their purposes—if, indeed, they had these purposes—in unequivocal language. So important was the office of president regarded that practically all of Article II was devoted to it. A single short paragraph dealt with the critical matter of a president's "death, resignation, or inability to discharge the powers and duties of the said office."

Should such a contingency arise—God forbid!—instructions for dealing with it were crammed into a single phrase: " . . . the same (power and duties of the said office) shall devolve on the vice-president."

In April, 1789, sixty-nine electors from ten states unanimously voted to place George Washington at the head of the new nation. Eight more presidents and fifty-two years later the unexpected happened; for the first time, a president died in office and it became immediately urgent to rally behind a successor.

John Tyler of Virginia occupied the place of vice-president largely because dominant men in the Whig party—and the rank and file of voters—regarded Tyler as harmless and the vice-presidency as an office with little honor and less power. Henry Clay and Daniel Webster were the two Whigs to watch. Both wanted and expected to win the presidency sooner or later; both had strong and vocal followings.

On inauguration day, 1841, Tyler took the oath of office first—in order to clear the decks for the really important ceremony, the inauguration of President Harrison. As soon as formalities were over and decency permitted, Tyler left the capital for his Williamsburg home: "very large and very airy and pleasant, fronting on a large lawn and surrounded by a most beautiful garden." Clearly he expected to spend most of the next four years in Williamsburg.

Just twenty days after he took office, Harrison suffered a severe attack of pneumonia. As his strength waned, it became apparent that he would die. No one thought it necessary to inform Tyler of the situation, however. Very early on the morning of April 5 he was awakened by loud banging on his front door. He went to the door in his nightshirt and admitted two couriers who informed him that President Harrison had died the day before. (The typically American legend that has the vice-president on his knees in the yard playing marbles with his son when he received the message, though widely circulated, is a folk myth without foundation.)

A terse written communication to Tyler from members of the cabinet addressed him, significantly, as "Mr. *Vice-President*." But one of the messengers was Daniel Webster's son Fletcher—who came in his capacity of chief clerk in the State Department. As clearly as anyone in the nation, Daniel Webster realized that his long-time rival, Henry Clay, now had an unmatched opportunity to move into the president's house for in the Whig convention of 1839, Clay had received 103 votes to Harrison's 94 on the first ballot. Webster had a strong following but had they been matched against one another then, Clay would have defeated the famous Massachusetts orator, hands down.

Precisely who chose Fletcher Webster to bear the news of Harrison's death to Tyler ambiguous records of the era do not say. But it was of crucial importance to Webster's ambitions that Tyler seize the presidency before Clay could lay claim to it. Hence it can hardly have been accidental or coincidental that Webster's son was sent to Williamsburg.

Within less than two hours after he got the news from Washington, Tyler was in the saddle for the first stage of his lightning-fast trip to the capital. Fletcher Webster and his companion as courier, a Mr. Beall who was on the payroll of the Senate, accompanied the vice-president. In Richmond, a special train was waiting. They reached Washington about 4 a.m. on April 6—and found the city buzzing with rumors and questions.

Tyler—who may have made up his mind independently or who may have been fed ideas and arguments by Fletcher Webster—acted promptly and decisively. At noon he went to the parlor of Brown's "Indian Queen" hotel and was sworn into the office of president by William Cranch, chief judge of the circuit court of the District of Columbia.

Whatever else may be concluded about the matter, this much is beyond dispute: no one had ever bothered seriously to try to determine whether death of a president in office should make the vice-president the chief executive, or merely an interim officer who would serve until a new president could be chosen. Language of the Constitution is ambiguous; "the same" may have meant to its framers the office of president, the duties of president—or both. Since the last surviving signer of the document had already died there was no one to question concerning the unwritten intent of its framers. With or without advice, Tyler had interpreted the document—and had acted in the light of his interpretation.

Henry Clay questioned the validity of Tyler's interpretation and was inclined to treat him as "acting president." In the House of Representatives, John McKeon of New York put in writing the question that was in every mind: "Is John Tyler entitled to the appellation 'President of the United States'?" Senator Allen of Ohio introduced a bill stipulating that in its communications with Tyler the lawmaking body should address him as "tl ɔ Vice-president, on whom, by the death of the late President, the powers and duties of the office of President have devolved." Both legislative moves to depose Tyler failed, but many national leaders echoed the sentiments of ex-President John Quincy Adams who was insistent that "a strict construction (of the Constitution) would warrant more than a doubt whether the Vice-president has the right to occupy the President's house, or to claim his salary, without an Act of Congress."

Fifty-one-year old Tyler, the youngest man who had so far assumed the office, made it clear that he had no intention to surrender it. "I am under providence made the instrument of a new test which is for the first time to be applied to our institutions," he wrote to Senator William C. Rives on April 9.

Vice-President Tyler's seizure of the nation's highest office, achieved with the encouragement and support of Daniel Webster, effectively settled the Constitutional question. In the light of the precedent he established, it became taken for granted that the vice-president becomes chief executive when the highest office in the land is vacated by death or by resignation.

Presiding over the Supreme Court in a case that involved appointment of a justice of the peace, John Marshall made the Court the final interpreter of the U.S. Constitution

Awesome Power of the U.S. Supreme Court Was Largely Created by John Marshall in One Uncontested Ruling

Americans today take it for granted that the U.S. Supreme Court has absolute authority to decide what the Constitution means and what can or cannot be done as a result of that meaning. Founding fathers left no evidence whatever that they envisioned such a role for the judiciary body. It has come to be accepted because a single astute ruling by John Marshall, uncontested at the time, established the court he headed as interpreter of the Constitution.

Marshall's decision was a knock-out punch in a long and bitter political fight. From the perspective of nearly two centuries it is delightfully incongruous that the most important single ruling ever made by the Supreme Court was issued in the course of settling a dispute over the post of justice of the peace in the District of Columbia.

Defeat of John Adams and the Federalists in the election of 1800 added fuel to a fire already raging. Thomas Jefferson and the Democratic-Republicans would control the executive and legislative branches—but Adams had many weeks in which to strengthen already powerful Federalist forces within the judicial branch of the youthful nation.

Under Adams' prodding and coaxing, Congress provided for the appointment of sixteen new federal circuit judges—along with the necessary marshals and other officials. A separate statute empowered the president to name forty-two justices of the peace, who would be needed when the nation's capital moved from Philadelphia to the District of Columbia.

As yet the U.S. Supreme Court had little prestige. Justices were required to serve in federal circuit courts as well as the high court, to which only a trickle of cases went. Nothing in the Constitution pre-scribes the number of Supreme Court justices. Originally set at six by Congress, the number had been enlarged to seven in 1807. Fearing that the seat occupied by a justice about to retire would be filled by a Jeffersonian Republican, Adams persuaded Congress to sidestep that calamity by stipulating that when vacated the post would not be filled. As a final move aimed at political stalemate if not checkmate, when the Chief Justice offered his resignation because of "poor health" late in 1800 the president accepted it. Then he named his own Secretary of State—who had never held a judicial post—to the vacant seat. Instead of leaving the cabinet to assume the bench, John Marshall was for a short time both Secretary of State and Chief Justice.

March 3, 1801, was Adams' last day in the White House. He worked methodically until the very end, signing commissions. Most of them named Federalists to judicial posts ranging from federal circuits to J.P. courts in the District of Columbia. Signed commissions were sent to the State Department where Secretary of State John Marshall supervised the affixing of the great seal to each. All of the important ones were then delivered. But, somehow, Secretary of State Marshall failed to see that commissions reached newly-named justices of the peace.

A few hours later, Chief Justice John Marshall administered the oath of office to Jefferson. Within days the new president, already seething at the way in which Adams had packed the judiciary, learned that J.P. commissions signed by his predecessor had never been delivered. He therefore worked with his Attorney General, Levi Lincoln, to prepare a new and smaller list of appointees to capital posts. Instead of forty-two justices of the peace to function in the District of Columbia, Jefferson named thirty—half of whom were given authority in Alexandria County. Of the thirty he named, twenty-three came from the Adams list.

Most men nudged out of comfortable five-year posts because of Marshall's oversight and the coming of a new regime accepted their fate. Forty-one-year-old William Marbury did not. He enlisted three other "midnight judges," Messrs. Harper, Hooe, and Ramsay. With their backing, he filed suit aimed at requiring the new Secretary of State, James Madison, to deliver the commissions that had been signed by Adams late in his last night as president. The suit went to the Supreme Court, headed by John Marshall, under provisions of the Judiciary Act of 1789.

Jefferson and the Democratic-Republic Congress reacted to Adams' many judicial appointments swiftly and violently. The statute creating sixteen new federal circuits was repealed and appointees were left jobless. To prevent any abrupt action by the jurists whom Marshall headed, Congress abolished the last session of the Supreme Court scheduled to be held in Philadelphia and stipulated that the body would not again convene until February, 1801—in Washington.

Marbury vs. Madison, as the suit revolving about grievances of a would-be justice of the peace came to be called, seemed to offer two alternatives. The Supreme Court could bow to the power of the executive branch and declare the Jefferson commissions valid. Or the court could hold the Adams appointments to be binding—and watch, helpless to do anything, as Jefferson and his key men blithely ignored the ruling of the court.

Not yet seasoned in his judiciary role, John Marshall nevertheless groped for—and found—the Achilles' heel of his political rivals. Presiding over a Supreme Court made up only of himself, Justice Samuel Chase and Justice Bushrod Washington, Marshall personally hammered out a lengthy opinion that—on the surface—seemed to limit the authority of the judicial body.

William Marbury and his co-plaintiffs, said the decision, were as a matter of law entitled to their commissions. But the high court could do nothing on their behalf; the section of the Judiciary Act of 1789 under which they had brought action was unconstitutional. The case of *Marbury vs. Madison* was received by the Supreme Court on February 3; hearings concluded on February 14; Marshall handed down the verdict on February 24.

Nothing in the Constitution itself gave the Supreme Court authority to serve as the definitive interpreter. English common law, on which the whole edifice of American law was based, offered no precedent for Marshall's ruling. Yet it evoked no public outcry. Even Thomas Jefferson said nothing in public. Writing to Mrs. Adams many months later (in September, 1804) the chief executive did protest that "The opinion which gives to the judges the right to decide what laws are constitutional, and what not, . . . would make the judiciary a despotic branch."

Unchallenged and untested, the ruling stood. There would be no similar one for another fifty-four years. By then, time and precedent had done their work. Chief Justice Marshall, pondering issues in which Secretary of State Marshall had been deeply involved, had at one stroke effectively hamstrung both the legislative and the executive branches of the government in matters involving constitutionality.

Delivery of that stroke was made possible because otherwise-forgotten William Marbury refused to accept the verdict when informed that he would not receive his promised commission as justice of the peace.

Units of the 51st New York and 51st Pennsylvania made the first Union crossing of Antietam Bridge

A Soldier's Love for Tobacco Helped Union Forces Protect the U.S. Capital from Attack by Confederate Forces

By mid-September, 1862, most Americans knew that an all-important clash between Union and Confederate forces was in the making. His recent victory at Bull Run had convinced Robert E. Lee that this was the time to invade Maryland.

Several motives prompted such a military move. Maryland herself seemed to be swaying in the balance; she might throw her weight toward the Confederate side if captured. The state was rich in resources, and Lee's army was badly in need of provisions. Most important of all, Washington was within easy striking distance of strategic

Maryland sites. If the capital could be captured, Britain or France or both might enter the war on the Confederate side.

Lee's tired but confident columns moved into Maryland and occupied the town of Frederick without opposition. Cavalrymen under Wade Hampton were billeted in and about the community. Meanwhile, Lee dispatched a force of 25,000 men in gray to capture Harper's Ferry—vital to seizure of the Shenandoah Valley. Other large units of Confederate troops moved toward Hagerstown, Maryland.

Lee's opponent, McClellan, was notoriously slow and indecisive. It would not be too great a gamble, Lee reasoned, to disperse his troops in the best positions for offensive moves. An attack by slow moving McClellan was practically unthinkable—totally out of character.

But a soldier's love for tobacco brought a sudden and dramatic change in the complex sitution.

Men in blue moved into Frederick, Maryland, on September 12 only a few hours after Confederate forces evacuated the area. After breaking ranks and preparing to make camp in a field outside the town, men fighting to preserve the Union were permitted to fan out for a rest period. Two of them strolled along the edge of a field vacated a few hours earlier by their foes. As they walked, one spied what looked like a bundle of cigars.

Tobacco was already becoming scarce, so cigars would be a real prize. Seized and examined, the bundle was found to include "three good 'uns" that were wrapped in what appeared to be a letter. According to the wrapping paper, it had come from "Headquarters, Army of Northern Virginia" just three days earlier.

Tobacco-hungry soldiers temporarily lost interest in the weed. Scanning the document in which their cigars were wrapped they found it to be addressed to Major General D. H. Hill—and to be signed by Assistant Adjutant General R. H. Chilton. Hastily passed upward through the chain of command, the tobacco wrapper reached the tent of General George B. McClellan late in the afternoon. Aides familiar with Chilton's handwriting pronounced the document to be genuine—a copy of "Special Order #191" giving detailed instructions to Lee's scattered forces.

Few formal accounts of the Battle of Antietam give the tobacco wrapper more than passing attention. Brigadier General Willard Webb, for example, says only that "through fortuitous circumstances" McClellan learned where Lee's units were located and what they had been ordered to do.

Special Order #191, used by a tobacco-loving Confederate officer to protect three precious cigars and accidentally dropped where Union soldiers could find it, brought radical changes in McClellan. Contrary to what his own men as well as his opponents knew to be his pattern of action, he moved swiftly and decisively.

Attacking at several points simultaneously, the Union commander reached the main body of Lee's troops at a point where Antietam Creek flows through a ravine near the village of Sharpsburg. September 17, 1862, eventually entered history as "the bloodiest single day of the war." Neither force was able to give a precise account of losses, but by the most conservative estimates at least 25,000 men fell dead or wounded on that day.

Some units crossed the creek by means of an old stone bridge. Many more forded Antietam. Only the lucky few—such as men detailed to man observation towers some distance from the actual hand-to-hand fighting—spent the day without danger.

Military historians tend to label Antietam as "a drawn battle" or as "a defeat for both armies." But it was this battle that stopped Lee's move to encircle and capture Washington. Having repulsed the attempt at invasion, Union leaders could realistically claim a major victory. In the glow of that victory Abraham Lincoln issued the preliminary draft

Signal tower on Elk Mountain, overlooking Antietam Battlefield

Abraham Lincoln visited Antietam Battlefield in October, 1862

of the Emancipation Proclamation. Only a few weeks later he personally visited the battlefield where the surging lines of Confederates had been stopped.

Had tobacco-hungry men in blue not grabbed those three cigars, there would have been no Battle of Antietam. It was McClellan's use of the set of Confederate orders that brought forces into head-on conflict and elevation of Union morale because Lee had been stopped.

It took weeks for news of the standoff and of the resulting Emancipation Proclamation to reach Europe. Confederate leaders did not wait to receive dispatches couched in diplomatic language, but concluded that they must fight it out alone. For the night after paper used to wrap three precious cigars brought 110,000 men into hand-to-hand conflict, it was clear that there would be no Confederate triumph of such magnitude that foreign intervention would help to divide America into two separate nations.

Typhoid Carrier Mary Mallon Stoutly Resisted Medical Treatment, Infected so Many Persons that Her Name Lives

Few persons are familiar with the story of Mary Mallon. But her nickname, "Typhoid Mary," is familiar throughout the English-speaking world. When she was found to have a low-level case of the dread fever that made her infectious, or a "carrier," she bluntly refused medical treatment—and went to great lengths to avoid having it forced upon her.

Even after she knew that she could transmit fever, Mary Mallon worked in several dozen private homes and public eating places under assumed names. Seven typhoid epidemics have been linked with her; how many others she triggered during years when she stayed underground, no one knows.

George A. Soper, a sanitary engineer, played the role of detective in one of the most bizarre of all medical dramas. A sanitary engineer who worked for the New York City Department of Health, Soper was consulted by a wealthy New Yorker late in 1906. Six guests at an Oyster Bay summer place had come down with typhoid; could the water on the place be contaminated—or perhaps the oysters that were taken from the bay?

Soper was called into the case very, very late—a full six months after the outbreak of the miniature epidemic. He eliminated all other possible factors, later reported that he "was reluctantly forced to the startling conclusion that the sudden rash of illness could only have been caused by a person—not by a thing."

Questioned in detail, banker Charles H. Warren remembered that they had changed cooks just before typhoid broke out among his guests. He had secured the cook—now long gone—through an employment agency. Warren remembered that she was about forty—give or take a year or two—and that she had blonde hair and blue eyes. "Her name was Mary Mallon, and that's all I know about her."

Soper assumed that it would be easy to locate the woman through the employment agency. He was wrong. Something had frightened her, and she was in hiding. Past records were scanty, but damning. Mary preferred to work for prosperous families, but changed jobs frequently. Interviews with past employers revealed that some of them had experienced outbreaks of typhoid. No one had any idea where the now-suspect woman might be found.

Soper began a door-to-door hunt in Park Avenue neighborhoods where his quarry had often worked. Early in March, 1907, he found her in a fashionable brownstone. She listened suspiciously while he explained his mission and told her that he'd have to get specimens of her urine and feces in order to run laboratory tests. Suddenly, without warning, the woman seized a big carving fork and brandished it. There was nothing the health officer could do but flee.

Located a few hours later in her rooming house, Mary Mallon began shouting at the top of her lungs. She never had typhoid! She was perfectly well! She wanted to be let alone! Clearly, she had no intention of cooperating.

Dr. J. S. Baker next confronted the medical suspect on March 18, 1907. He brought along a court order requiring her to undergo examination—and was backed by three police officers. Still Mary Mallon escaped from them and hid for six hours in a closet.

Taken into custody, she was locked in an isolation ward at the Willard Parker Hospital for Contagious Diseases on East 16th Street. Drs. Robert L. Wilson and William H. Park ran a series of tests during a period of eight months. Though the woman was outwardly healthy, most of the time her stools were potent with bacteria. No doubt about it . . . she was a true carrier. Told of her condition, she flatly refused medical treatment that might free her of contamination.

Mary Mallon was transferred to a hospital on North Brother Island in the East River. By this time, newspapers had learned of the bizarre case and had tried—unsuccessfully—to interview her. In the headlines she came to be known simply as "Typhoid Mary."

Health officials gave her an ultimatum: she could submit to medical treatment—or spend the rest of her life in detention. Instead of accepting one of the two courses of action she found a lawyer who would take her case and unsuccessfully sued for freedom.

Officials became weary of the squabble, so in 1910 reached a formal agreement. In exchange for her release Mary Mallon swore she would give up cooking and handling of food. In addition, she would report to the Health Department every ninety days.

Once out of custody, she disappeared.

Using names like Mary Brown, Marie Breshof, and many others that were never uncovered she worked in the kitchens of clubs, hotels and restaurants. Suddenly the long-cold trail of the carrier became very hot. In February, 1915, the noted Sloane Hospital for Women was hit by typhoid; twenty-five nurses and attendants were stricken almost simultaneously.

Called into the case, George Soper examined personnel records. A cook hired not long before the outbreak had left without notice when someone jokingly called her Typhoid Mary. Examination of her handwriting left no doubt; the food handler who had left in a huff really was Mary Mallon.

Police tracked the fugitive to Long Island—and arrested her in the act of preparing a bowl of gelatin for a friend. She was taken back to North Brother Island in March, 1915, and was kept there until her death on November 11, 1938.

Always, she refused to answer questions or to take medicine. She never consented to removal of her gall bladder (thought to harbor the bacteria that passed continuously from her body) or to be photographed. She did learn some techniques of laboratory work and during her latter years drew $60 a month as an inmate technician in the hospital to which she was confined.

No one knows how many persons were infected by food that she handled. During the handful of years in which her activities were traced, seven separate epidemics of fever were linked with her. Some public health authorities guessed her toll of victims to be "a few hundred;" others insisted that it exceeded one thousand.

Publicity about the mystery woman who wouldn't accept medical help led to identification of numerous other typhoid carriers—all of whom cooperated and received treatment. This factor plus improvement in sanitary conditions took from the list of major killers in the U.S. the disease that gave Typhoid Mary the title that became a household term.

Steamer LEXINGTON as depicted in "The Extra Sun," lithograph by Currier

A Forgotten Disaster Was the Springboard that Enabled Currier & Ives to Leap into the Place of "Printmakers to the American People"

Except to serious collectors of prints the name "Currier & Ives" is likely to suggest gentle pastoral scenes, celebrities of a bygone era, fine horses and elegant clipper ships. The firm's own "Catalogue of Popular Cheap Prints containing nearly Eleven hundred subjects" listed additional categories: "Juvenile, Domestic, Love Scenes, Kittens and Puppies, Ladies Heads, Catholic Religious, Patriotic, Landscapes, Vessels, Comic, School Rewards and Drawing Studies, Flowers and Fruits, Motto Cards, Horses, Family Registers, Memory Pieces and Miscellaneous in great variety."

45

That bland list gives no hint that Nathaniel Currier began depicting disasters very early or that he was propelled into the national limelight through skillful—and astute—exploitation of the 1840 loss of the steamer *Lexington* in Long Island Sound.

Regarded as a marvel of the shipbuilding art when she was launched in 1835, the *Lexington*—all 205 feet of her—came into existence through the bustling genius of Cornelius Vanderbilt. Because he operated a fleet of passenger ships Vanderbilt was dubbed "Commodore" in 1837 by the *Journal of Commerce*—a title that stuck to him when he turned from water to the rails.

The *Lexington* involved a major gamble for the boat owner who was eager to become a business tycoon. Passenger business between New York and Providence, Rhode Island, was a virtual monopoly of the wealthy and powerful Boston and New York Transportation Co. To challenge it, Vanderbilt went in hock for all he had, built the 488-ton *Lexington,* and advertised her as "the fastest boat in the world." She did make sixteen miles an hour under good weather conditions, and gave established lines real trouble. To stifle competition from a third line, the Atlantic Steamboat Co., the Boston-based firm offered to give Vanderbilt a profit of nearly $20,000 if he would sell his fine, fast vessel. Had Vanderbilt not taken that 1839 offer, he might have died unknown. For direct losses plus lawsuits resulting from the *Lexington* tragedy amounted to more than $2,000,000—many times Vanderbilt's assets in 1840.

Bound for Stonington, Connecticut, with a crew of forty and about one hundred passengers, the *Lexington* left New York on the evening of January 13, 1840. Fire broke out as the vessel nosed through Long Island Sound. Crewmen turned back toward the pier, but the fire was raging out of control while the *Lexington* was still two miles from land. A few persons managed to stay afloat on bales of cotton that had constituted the cargo. But an estimated 136 burned to death or perished in the icy water.

Just three days after the tragedy New Yorkers were offered a chance to buy a lithograph print of the burning ship accompanied by seven columns of description in fine print. Termed "The Extra Sun" and issued under auspices of The New York *Sun* it is widely regarded as the first illustrated extra in history. Buyers who were impressed by the vivid illustration that headed the page could look beneath it and discover that it was drawn by W. K. Hewitt and produced by "N. Currier, Lith. & Pub. 2 Spruce St. N.Y."

Colored litho prints of the burning of New York's famous Crystal Palace on October 5, 1858, were just 6¢ per copy, wholesale, from the firm that started a national sales program with a disaster and depicted a great many notable ones

"The Extra Sun" was first a local and then a national triumph. Profits from it gave Currier the opportunity he had been seeking to distribute his prints on a more than local basis. Publicity about it assured him of a market for whatever he could produce.

Currier's move to capitalize on the disaster did not occur in a vacuum. Already the Massachusetts native who had learned the trade as an apprentice in Boston had discovered that there is money in violent death. Two of his earliest surviving prints, both uncolored, had enjoyed local success. One of them shows "Ruins of the Planters Hotel, New-Orleans, Which fell at two O'clock, on the Morning of the 15th of May 1835, burying 50 persons, 40 of which escaped with their Lives." Another depicts "Ruins of the Merchant's Exchange, N.Y., after the Destructive Conflagration of Decbr. 16 & 17, 1835."

Compared with "The Extra Sun" these and all earlier Currier prints were small-time stuff. A biographer of the printer may have been overenthusiastic in declaring that "overnight N. Currier became a national institution," but there's no doubt that his illustrated account of the burning of the *Lexington* put him head and shoulders above all competitors who operated on a local basis.

Nathaniel's brother Charles worked with him for a period. Then Charles' brother-in-law, native New Yorker James M. Ives, entered the business a decade after publication of "The Extra Sun." Ives soon became a full partner and the firm name was changed to the universally familiar "Currier & Ives."

Black-and-white prints produced by means of a special kind of soft and very porous stone imported from Bavaria were hand-tinted by crews of women who worked on long waist-high tables. Production costs were kept so low that except for special editions and large folio prints the typical product that bore the "Currier & Ives" imprint was sold at about 6¢, in quantity.

For more than half a century, Currier & Ives prints depicted every aspect of life in America. Though not given a separate section in the publishers' catalog, many best-sellers capitalized on the news value of shipwrecks, fires, train wrecks, and other disasters.

Development of photography and photoengraving gave Currier & Ives little trouble at first. But as the arts progressed and illustrated weeklies began to be widely distributed, hand-tinted lithographed prints became harder and harder to sell. Hundreds of thousands of them were discarded as trash before they began to be collectors' items early in this century. By 1928 one rare print depicting "The Life of a Hunter—A Tight Fix" was worth $3,000.

Widely known as "Printmakers to the American Nation," Currier & Ives didn't keep precise records. No one knows how many separate prints they issued, but the number is believed to range above or below 4000. Only harum-scarum Charles, Nathaniel's brother and part-time business colleague bothered to keep specimens of a majority of the later prints. He did it because he had convenient storage space for proofs.

In a unique sense, Currier & Ives prints *are* 19th-century America. Proud owners of prints that show trotting horses, Biblical scenes, and the American countryside might never have had an opportunity to acquire them had not the *Lexington* gone down in flames.

President Grover Cleveland—who won the White House in spite of scandals greater than those that have defeated other aspirants

Three Separate Stains on His Record, Each Enough to Keep a Man Out of the White House, Failed to Stop Grover Cleveland

Stephen Grover Cleveland was practically unknown nationally when Democrats nominated him for president in July, 1884. Meeting at Exposition Hall in Chicago, jubilant delegates dubbed the man they chose on the second ballot as "Grover the Good."

But because they had made only the most perfunctory inquiry into his background, elation of Democratic leaders was short-lived. In quick succession the man who had stepped into the limelight was confronted by three separate stains on his record.

Son of a Presbyterian minister, Cleveland was born on March 18,

49

1837, in Caldwell, New Jersey, as the fifth of nine children. His father got the job of district secretary for the American Home Missionary Society, which required the family to move to the village of Holland Patent in central New York. At sixteen Grover, who had already stopped using his first name, was thrown on his own by the death of his father.

He went to New York City job hunting, and for a time worked at a school for the blind. Then he got a post as clerk in a Buffalo law firm. He studied at night, sometimes without sleeping at all, and learned enough law to win admission to the bar in 1859.

He was moderately successful as an attorney, but when the post of sheriff of Erie County became vacant in 1870 he ran for the job. "No other lawyer would have considered the post suitably dignified for his talents," a local newspaper editorial commented in reporting that the attorney had won by 303 votes.

After three years as sheriff Cleveland joined the firm of Bass and Bissell and again became a full-time lawyer. He nearly doubled his weight from beer and sausages at Schenkelberger's Restaurant. Civic corruption encouraged him to run for mayor in 1881. He won, and established a local reputation as a reformer. This gave him a base from which to win the governorship of New York in 1882.

Two years later Republicans chose as their national standard-bearer James G. Blaine of Maine. He would be difficult if not impossible to beat. Democrats, who decided that their best hope lay in "a new face," rallied to the support of Cleveland as "a man who has never even set foot in Washington."

Within ten days after being nominated, Cleveland moved from obscurity into national notoriety.

Republicans had no difficulty digging out his record as sheriff of Erie County—and learning that he had presided over the executions of condemned killers Patrick Morrissey and Jack Gaffney. Regardless of offenses committed by the executed men, two hangings were enough to serve as a hook on which to display the emotion-charged label: "The Hangman."

While broadsides about "The Hangman" were still being printed and distributed a second scandal broke over the head of the man who hadn't really sought the nomination. In its issue of July 21, 1884, the Buffalo, New York *Evening Telegram* gave front-page space to "A Terrible Tale."

According to that tale, the candidate for the presidency had long been involved with Maria Halpin. "A child was born out of holy wedlock," readers were informed. "Now ten years of age, this sturdy lad is named Oscar Folsom Cleveland. He and his mother have been supported in part by our ex-mayor who now aspires to the White House. Astute readers may put the facts together and draw their own conclusions."

When the story broke, frantic Democratic leaders wired Cleveland for instructions. His telegram became a classic document in American politics. "Tell the truth!" Cleveland said.

The truth, it developed, was that Cleveland and other men had visited Maria Halpin regularly. As the only bachelor in the group Cleveland took financial responsibility for the child. "The boy could be mine," he confessed, "I do not know." National Music Co. of Chicago promptly published and Republican money subsidized mass distribution of a song unique in the annals of American politics. "Ma! Ma! Where's My Pa?" made it impossible for any informed voter to be unaware of scandal in Cleveland's past.

Just to make sure that the big man was properly polished off, opponents dragged a third skeleton out of his closet. Called to the colors to help save the Union, Cleveland had resorted to provisions of the Conscription Act of 1863. Under its terms he had paid $150 for a substitute who would wear Union blue—while he remained in his handsome residence and office building.

Cleveland made no serious national effort to inform voters that at the time he bought his way out of the army he already had two brothers in uniform—plus a mother and two sisters at home to support. His indifference to the charge was characteristic. Unlike modern candidates, he never mounted a serious campaign. He made few public appearances and fewer speeches. While charges echoed and re-echoed, he stayed at his desk in Albany and looked after his work as governor.

Experts on both sides conceded that New York was the pivotal state—and scandals were expected to beat him there. That might have been the case had not political foes made one last effort to milk the paternity issue for all it was worth. Just a week before the election Blaine himself went to New York City and met with clergymen who were already indignant that a man so stained as Cleveland might become president.

Buffalo, New York, residence and law office of Grover Cleveland, Esq.

The Rev. S. D. Burchard, pastor of Murray Hill Presbyterian church, was spokesman for the clergy. While reporters jotted down notes he talked earnestly with Blaine. In the midst of the conversation he referred to the Democratic Party as "the party of Rum, Romanism, and Rebellion." Blaine made no objection to the allusion.

"Rum, Romanism, and Rebellion" made headlines in most New York papers on October 29 and 30, however. Angry Irish Catholics turned out in record numbers to repudiate the man who had permitted a slur at their faith. Ten days after the election Republican leaders conceded defeat; Cleveland had carried New York State (and hence the nation) by 1149 popular votes. Nationally he had less than fifty percent of the votes in the four-way race, but in the electoral college he took 219 votes to Blaine's 182.

Outcome of the hotly-contested election was apparent on the day Blaine's forces conceded that the "Rum, Romanism, and Rebellion" reference had brought out enough angry Catholics to swing the national contest. On learning that his opponents had finally conceded, the candidate plagued by scandal admitted reporters to his Albany office. "I am glad they have conceded," the big man said. "Very glad. There will be no trouble. If they had not conceded, I should have felt it my duty to take my seat anyhow."

The Selden Motorcar—built as a model early in this century and later given a backdated painted label—had a 2-cylinder, 4-cycle motor

George B. Selden: The Lawyer Who Patented the Automobile

New York attorney George Baldwin Selden (1846-1922) never actually invented anything. But he had a keen imagination and was a good authority on patent law. As a result he managed to gain a legal monopoly on the manufacture of automobiles in the U.S. It held up long enough for him to collect at least $1,500,000 in royalties. Then it was challenged by hard-headed young Henry Ford of Detroit, who broke the monopoly during the years he was surging to first place among automakers.

Discharged from the Union Army in 1865, 19-year-old Selden had entered Yale Sheffield Scientific School, but during his second year his father's illness forced him to drop out of school. Reluctantly he decided to follow in his father's footsteps and hang out his shingle as a lawyer.

Admitted to the bar in 1871, young Selden continued to tinker with mechanical contrivances such as those he had studied in engineering school. Beginning in 1875, he designed several types of engines; none worked.

Petroleum technicians were just beginning to achieve success in separating the liquid into specific fractions. Selden decided that one of the fractions was the fuel of the future—and that he must have a monopoly on "gasoline road locomotives." His decision was triggered by a visit to the Philadelphia Centennial Exposition of 1876. There he saw a two-cycle gasoline motor, designed and patented by George B. Brayton.

Selden knew enough law—and engineering—to believe that a three-cycle motor would get around the Brayton patent. So he returned to Rochester and had a 600-pound engine built. To save time and money, only one of the three cylinders was bored and fitted with a piston. Theoretically, though, the "Selden engine" ought to operate at 500 rpm as opposed to 25 rpm for the Brayton engine.

By 1877, Selden was ready to make his first legal move. He drew a sketch of a gasoline-powered vehicle with a crude friction clutch and a system for changing gears.

U.S. law of the era provided that the holder of a patent was entitled to a monopoly during a period of seventeen years. There was no provision for renewal. Since no one was actually building and selling automobiles based on the Selden concept, it would have been a mistake to take out a patent too early. George Selden waited almost two years before he even applied for a patent. Once the application was on file, he began adding new claims. When patent examiners disallowed a particular claim, he was given two years to alter his application—and add more claims. Until a patent was actually granted, only the applicant and the U.S. Patent Office knew anything about it. But date of the first application was used in establishing priority. George Brayton, inventor of the engine that Selden modified slightly, later said of his competitor: "He was a punk engineer—but a damned smart patent lawyer! He knew exactly what to do and, when."

1894 was a break-through year. The world's first automobile race was run from Paris to Rouen. Publicity about it helped to convince many members of the public that the horseless carriage, which had run eighty miles at ten miles per hour, might really make a go of it.

It was time to quit stalling, Selden decided. He abandoned legal maneuvers and asked the U.S. Patent Office to give him a seventeen-year monopoly on the manufacture and sale of gasoline-powered vehicles. Patent #549, 160 was issued on November 5, 1895. A few months later Charles and Frank Duryea claimed the first U.S. commercial sale of a horseless carriage powered by gasoline.

During this era the world's largest maker of bicycles was the Pope Manufacturing Co. of Hartford, Connecticut. Col. Albert A. Pope, self-made millionaire who owned the company and the trademark "Columbia," calculated that in time the horseless carriage might cut into the bicycle market. So he decided to build and market a car that he would call "Columbia."

Pope hired a bright young engineer named Hiram Percy Maxim (1869-1936) and told him to put crews to work in order to get gasoline-powered vehicles into production. By 1897, ten Columbias were in various stages of completion.

It was then that a member of Colonel Pope's legal department discovered that they were too late. "A man named Selden has already won a patent," he told his employer. "I have checked the records carefully. He has an airtight case. We could fight, but we couldn't win."

Pope had made his millions by shrewd moves that included the principle, "If you can't lick your foes, then join them." He sent for Selden, worked out an agreement by which the all-inclusive patent would be assigned to a holding company in return for a percentage of all royalties collected.

Pope had the right connections to make a go of the Electric Vehicle Company. Stockholders who bought into it included some of America's top financiers. William C. Whitney, former Secretary of the Navy and a noted capitalist, was among the first to enter the company. He was joined by Thomas F. Ryan of New York and P. A. B. Widener of Philadelphia. Both men were already prominent as electric traction magnates. New York banker Anthony M. Brady provided more capital.

Once the Electric Vehicle Company gained rights to the Selden patent, officials announced that all gasoline-powered cars made in the U.S. would have to be built by license—accompanied by royalties of

5% of retail price. Suits against the Buffalo Gasoline Motor Company and the Automobile Fore-carriage Co. were won easily. Sued for infringement of the Selden patent, the big and growing Winton Motor Carriage Co. capitulated and took a consent decree.

Repeatedly sustained in courts, the Selden interests clearly had the U.S. auto industry by the tail. Firms licensed to operate under the Selden patent formed the Association of Automobile Makers. Every car produced carried a plate acknowledging that it was made by license.

Practically all manufacturers joined the Association—but one stubbornly refused to do so. Henry Ford, head of the hold-out organization, was just sixteen at the time attorney George Selden filed his preliminary application for a patent in 1879. Suit was filed against Ford's company on October 22, 1903, in the Southern District of New York.

It looked like an open-and-shut case. Members of the Association of Automobile Makers represented more than $70,000,000 in capital assets. During 1903, Ford's working capital was just under $30,000.

Both parties to the suit began taking out newspaper and magazine advertisements while the case was being fought. A full-page ad in *The*

George B. Selden, who was a better lawyer than engineer, donned mechanic's clothing for workshop photos, taken about 1909

Automobile warned that "the basic Selden patent will be enforced against all infringers." Meanwhile, The Ford Motor Co. bought space to tell prospective dealers, users, and exporters: "We will protect you against all prosecution from alleged infringements. No court in the U.S. has ever decided in favor of the patent; all that has been done is to record a prior agreement between parties."

Litigation dragged out for a period of six years. Testimony in the case filled thirty-six volumes. In September, 1909, the court of New York's Southern District upheld the Selden patent. This verdict was based, in part, upon physical examination of a car hastily manufactured by engineer Henry Cave—who worked from Selden's initial drawings. The gasoline vehicle he made never ran more than fourteen hundred feet. Boldly labelled "1877" in spite of having been put together more than thirty years after that date, it helped to sway judicial opinion.

Federal Judge Charles M. Hough, who handed down the ruling supporting the claims of Selden, said that "this American patent represents a great idea shaped in 1879, which lay fallow in a Patent Office file wrapper until 1895."

Henry Ford promptly appealed the decision. During the two years in which arguments were being heard, the Detroit manufacturer's arguments with Selden interests were repeatedly aired in the press. In all history, no patent fight has been given so much free coverage.

January, 1911, brought the case to a close. Selden's patents were still valid, the courts declared. But his combination of engine, running gear, clutch, and other components did not cover the "modern" automobile. That meant that the Model T did not represent an infringement upon the patent covering a car never manufactured.

Attorney Selden was not greatly disturbed. His monopoly had just one more year to run. Royalties from a paper invention had made him comfortable for life. Consequently the attorney rejected suggestions that the case be taken to the Supreme Court. Until the end of his life, in 1922, his investments returned more than adequate income for his needs. He died insisting that though he never actually built an automobile, he was the inventor of "the idea of the gasoline-propelled vehicle."

The ghost of Charles I, as depicted in a 1659 pamphlet, may have tormented the "regicides" who escaped to the New World—but if so, they failed to show remorse

For 20 Years, Pious New England Puritans Sheltered Fugitives in an International Manhunt

During 17th-century civil wars in England, the victory of Oliver Cromwell made King Charles I a political prisoner. Recaptured after an escape that may have been engineered by Cromwell himself, the king was brought before a High Court of Justice whose members were so biased that they constituted a rigged jury. Some balked at putting their ex-king to death, but fifty-nine followers of Cromwell put their names to the death warrant.

Failure of Cromwell's Commonwealth and restoration of the monarchy brought inevitable retaliation against the regicides—whom the new Parliament branded as "unpardonable." Each man held responsible for the death of Charles was subject to being hanged, or drawn and quartered while still alive. With a price upon his head, every fugitive was a prototype of the 20th-century war criminal—safe nowhere, and doomed to live in hiding for the remainder of his days.

Three of these wanted men fled to New England and found sanctuary among pious Puritans. Throughout the region there was an unwritten conspiracy to shelter the regicides—in the name of God and at the risk of being seized and condemned as a traitor to the crown. At least one colonial governor was a party to the plot. The Rev. Increase Mather of Boston's North Church plunged into it with such holy zeal that he served as intermediary through whom code letters were exchanged between fugitives and their loved ones in England. Spurning the bounty offered by agents of King Charles II and risking their own lives by harboring fugitives, Puritans stuck together so closely that all three regicides who fled to the colonies died of natural causes.

Years earlier, in England, only a handful of persons were really eager to see Charles' head roll. Many who helped to unseat him from the throne would have been satisfied to see him banished to a land where he could do no harm, or at most confined in a comfortable prison for life. Oliver Cromwell wrestled with the issue and concluded that in order to make the world safe for the "Saints" of whom he was chief, the ex-monarch must die. Publicly, he asked his followers to wait patiently for a sign from God.

Ten days after Cromwell included such a plea in his speech to the Army Council on November 1, 1647, Charles escaped from Hampton Court where he had been under detention. Edward Whalley, commander of a regiment of horse and first cousin to Cromwell, was responsible for guarding the king. Much evidence, including a letter from Cromwell to Whalley, suggests that his captors deliberately permitted the monarch to escape in order to find a temporary haven on the Isle of Wight.

Now Cromwell had his sign from heaven! Now he had an issue on which to base his demand that Charles be tried for his life. Writing to Lord Wharton on January 1, 1651, Cromwell urged: "Be not offended at the manner of God's working; perhaps no other way was left." That constituted a theological argument after-the-fact; Charles had been dead for nearly two years.

Though the special High Court of Justice that heard the case against the king included 135 men, only 59 of them signed the death warrant. Cromwell's cousin was the fourth man to sign. William Goffe, son-in-law of Whalley and like him a major general who commanded a district of the Commonwealth, was fourteenth to sign. Two-thirds of the way down the list appeared the signature of John Dixwell.

Almost as soon as Charles was dead, the rank and file of Englishmen began to realize that with Cromwell at the head of the nation they had merely exchanged one harsh master for another. An informal program of beatification began, with the result that before he had been in his grave a decade the once-hated Charles I was revered as a sainted martyr.

This reversal of public opinion strengthened the hand of those who itched to topple Cromwell from power and of those who yearned for the good old days of monarchy. From his self-imposed exile Charles II crystallized national opion by declaring for a free Parliament and issuing a proclamation of General Amnesty. Under its terms, if made king he would punish no one except persons specified by Parliament.

When in 1660 it became clear that the monarchy would be restored, one-time major generals Edward Whalley and William Goffe managed to gain passage on the *Prudent Mary*—whose destination was the colonies. John Dixwell fled to the continent, remained in hiding there for a time, and then joined his comrades who were comfortably established in New England.

Over and over, officers of the crown sent their men on forced marches when they got wind of the whereabouts of one or more of the fugitives. Over and over, God-fearing and law-abiding Puritans hid the regicides, fed and clothed them, and helped them to find new havens. Though broadsides and proclamations repeatedly emphasized that there was a reward of £100 per man offered for the regicides, no colonist seems ever to have attempted to turn bounty hunter.

All three men used false names at times, but identities of all three were known to prominent men in Massachusetts and in Connecticut. Their New World hosts gave aid and comfort to the wanted men "for conscience' sake." They did it with such zealous effectiveness that John Dixwell, youngest of the fugitives and last to die, married twice and sired at least three children before his death at age eighty-one.

Dixwell was buried in New Haven close to the spot where Yale was later founded; his grave was marked with a stone that bore his initials. Goffe vanished for good during a 1679 manhunt; his father-in-

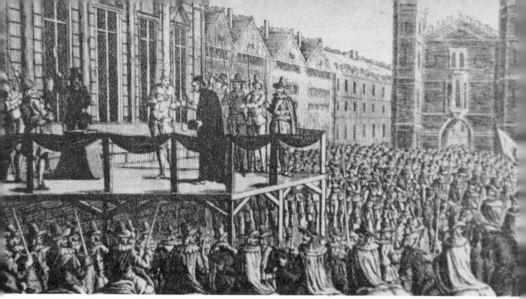

As he went to his execution on January 30, 1649, pious captors of Charles I informed him that "God did not wish him to escape"

law had already died of natural causes and had been buried in an unmarked grave.

Not even the long arm of the English king and the awesome power of his redcoats and colonial officers could shake the solidarity of Puritan New England. A twenty-year international manhunt for men condemned as murderers of Charles I failed to flush even one of the three into the hands of the law.

The 21-Year-Old Who Discovered a Continent

In November, 1820, the captain of a U.S. sealing ship discovered the Continent of Antarctica. It had been hunted for 200 years by veteran explorers—but at the time he made the find, Nathaniel Brown Palmer was just twenty-one years old.

Born in Stonington, Connecticut, on August 8, 1799, young Palmer practically grew up in his father's shipyard. At age fourteen Nat went to sea—as a blockade runner in the War of 1812. Three years later the boy whose acquaintances said "he had salt water in his veins" had become second mate of a deep-sea vessel. A year later, at age eighteen, Palmer got his own command—the schooner *Galena*.

Stonington was then the world center of the seal trade. At first casually and experimentally, New England whalers had begun to kill and skin a few of the animals. Pelts brought about $2 each. Even a small vessel could bring back 8,000 to 10,000 pelts, though. So sealing surged to prominence. Persons who invested in a successful voyage could expect profits ranging as high as 800 percent.

Fast growth in sealing, which involved Britain and Russia as well as the U.S., led to a rapid decline in the number of seals that lived in the old, established rookeries. This factor spurred an intensive search for a new source of seals.

For more than 200 years seamen had talked vaguely of a "Lost Aurora" believed to lie somewhere south of Cape Horn. Captain James

Cook and other noted explorers had spent months hunting for the semilegendary land, but none had succeeded in setting foot upon it.

Shrewd Yankee investors of Stonington reasoned that many seals must breed in regions south of islands that appeared on conventional navigational charts. In order to search for such islands, Connecticut businessmen outfitted their first voyage to search for Lost Aurora in 1817.

One of the men who made that voyage—which proved fruitless in terms of major discoveries—was Nathaniel Palmer. He went as second mate of the brig *Hersilia*. The post, which involved a demotion in rank, was taken because good prospects of a huge seal kill, with bounty to match, offered bigger reward than conventional captain's pay.

The *Hersilia* found no new land—but brought back to Stonington more than 10,000 prime pelts. Merchants and seamen of the city decided to send a much larger expedition into the general vicinity of the South Shetland Islands. By standards of the era, the expedition that left Stonington on July 31, 1820, was a huge convoy. Five brigs were included, along with three schooners.

As an extra precaution investors had commissioned the building of a special shallow-draft sloop. This forty-five ton vessel, about forty-seven feet long, had a draft of just six feet. She stood so low in the water that her decks were washed by waves more than eighteen inches high. Dubbed *Hero*, this sloop was something of an experiment in both shipbuilding and in sealing. Designed to serve as scout for the entire flotilla, the vessel could safely explore coastal regions in which ships of conventional build were likely to founder or to become stuck.

Nat Palmer, commander of the *Hero*, had just six men in his crew, but was assured of a captain's share of prize money from the sealing expedition. Along with other vessels of the Yankee flotilla, the *Hero* reached the South Shetland Islands in early November, but found no seals. Logs of the Stonington ships, carefully perused decades later, indicated that skippers believed sealers of other nations beat them to the region and had taken pups as well as adult seals.

There were two choices: go home empty, or look elsewhere. Captains held a council of war and decided that the big ships would wait while the *Hero* explored uncharted waters farther south.

November 16 saw the tiny sloop reach Deception Island—known by name to some navigators, but shunned because heavy fog made the waters dangerous. Palmer's shallow-draft vessel entered a previously unknown "spacious harbor with very deep water" that is now known to be the crater of an extinct volcano. Probably from the top of the mast of the tiny *Hero,* on a day "surprisingly clear," twenty-one-year-old Nathaniel Palmer was "thrown into great excitement upon seeing to the south a vast extent of land."

By late evening on the following day, November 17, the little sloop from Connecticut was close to what is now known as Trinity Island. The water, "filled with immense Ice Bergs," was extremely dangerous. Early next morning the youthful skipper guided his craft ten miles into a strait "tending SSW and NNE and Literally filled with Ice and the shore inaccessible."

Palmer, whose notes in the log are unusually terse, commented only that "We thought it not Prudent to venture farther . . . for everywhere, the shore was Perpendicular." The Stonington youth had no idea that he had discovered the last of the world's continents, or that its 5,000,000 square miles harbored penguins and other strange creatures—with ice perhaps covering vast treasures in oil and minerals.

Palmer went back to the sealing squadron and soon afterward led other ships into a bay in the Greenwich Islands, where seals were found in abundance. Again out scouting a few weeks later, on February 5, 1821, Palmer came across "strange vessels." He had found an expedition made up of two Russian sloops under the command of Captain Baron Fabian Gottlieb von Bellinghausen. Bellinghausen had been sent by Czar Alexander I "to search for the southern continent."

Later, in describing his brief meeting with the Americans, Bellinghausen told of the young skipper's discovery and referred to the region he found as Palmer's Land. It was through the influence of his Russian rival that the name of Palmer gained a place on the map.

Now known to extend about 700 miles from its base, the region is generally labelled the Palmer Peninsula. Most of the land surface is covered with an immense ice shelf, but under that ice lies a 13,700-foot mountain peak.

Nathaniel Palmer returned to Stonington more excited about the fact that the holds of their ships were bulging with seal skins than about his having reached the last unexplored outpost of our planet. He was master of a vessel that traded in the Spanish Main during 1822-26 and gained regional fame as designer of numerous noted packets and clipper ships. Returning from the Orient, he died in San Francisco on June 21, 1877, still unaware of the importance of the discovery he made at age twenty-one.

America's Greatest Wave of Addiction to "Hard" Drugs Was Triggered by . . . Military Doctors

At the midpoint of the last century, little was known about the long-range effects of narcotics. But opium and its derivatives were effective in easing pain, so "hard" drugs were universally used in military medicine during the Civil War. At war's end, conservative estimates suggest that at least 100,000 veterans—most of whom had fought for the Union—were addicted to opium as a result of battlefield treatment. Total population of the nation was then less than 40,000,000.

Civil War physicians regarded opium as helpful in treatment of dysentery and other common maladies, as well as in relief of intractable pain. So many soldiers used so much of it that civilian demand continued at a high level after hostilities ceased. In 1858 alone, the U.S. imported 71,839 pounds of the powerful narcotic derived from the poppy plant.

The official medicine pannier of the U.S. Army contained fifty-two bottles and vials. None had any marking except an identification number on the top of the cork. Physicians in uniform knew, however, that their basic kit included these drugs:

#14 - cough mixture with opium base
#21 - tincture of opium (often called laudanum)
#28 - paregoric
#33 - opium powder
#39 - morphine sulphate
#40 - pills of opium and camphor
#42 - pills of opium alone

A Confederate medicine wagon carried only twenty drugs in stock. Though prominent on the list, opium and morphine sulphate were often in short supply—hence men in gray ran much less risk of addiction than did their foes in blue.

Used as a painkiller, opium was administered in the form of pills, as a liquid (laudanum), as a camphorated tincture (paregoric), and as morphine. Pills and tinctures were swallowed. Much morphine sulphate was dusted directly into wounds.

At first the hypodermic needle saw little use on the battlefield. Perfected only in 1840, it was not generally familiar to physicians. But as fighting progressed the new instrument came into wider use—almost exclusively for administration of morphine.

In that era, the *U.S. Dispensatory,* or official list of approved drugs, classified opium as "a stimulant narcotic." It was believed to "increase the force, fullness, and frequency of the pulse, augment the temperature of the skin, invigorate the muscular system, quicken the senses, animate the spirits, and give new energy to the intellectual faculties."

Surgeon General Thomas Lawson, who headed the U.S.A. Medical Department at the outbreak of hostilities, had not kept up with the progress of research. He discouraged his officers from purchasing textbooks, doubted the usefulness of the clinical thermometer, and considered the stethoscope "a ridiculous plaything." Small wonder that under Lawson and his successors amputation became the surgical trademark of battlefield medicine.

Forward stations were supposed to be equipped with pails, basins, bandages, splints, and sponges—plus the three great drugs of the era: quinine, chloroform, and opium. Treatment of the wounded was often confined to checking hemorrhage and administering opiates laced with whisky. Most amputations took place in field hospitals, where wounded men received more opium.

Since ancient times it had been known that juice of the poppy, *Papaver somniferum,* relieves many symptoms linked with dysentery. Intestinal disturbances outnumbered all other Civil War maladies, combined. Official medical records of the Union Army list 1,155,266 admissions to sick report for acute diarrhea; 170,488 for chronic diarrhea; 233,812 for acute dysentery; and 25,670 for chronic dysentery.

Conditions in the Army of the Confederacy were even worse. During the first year of fighting, nearly two-thirds of the men in gray were incapacitated for weeks during recurring bouts with dysentery. Confederate medical officer Bedford Brown declared that "nine-tenths of all recruits were attacked by chronic diarrhoea."

In the sick bay as in the surgeon's tent, opium was the great cure-all. Men who had repeated bouts with dysentery, requiring increasingly larger doses with each illness, often became addicted without knowing how the craving was established.

A minority of physicians warned about dangers in promiscuous use of the narcotic. Sanford B. Hunt, M.D., voiced the majority opinion in a report on "Camp Diarrhaea and Dysentery." According to that report, "Opium is the one drug that at least alleviates the alvine flux, even if it does not cure."

Confederate demands for the drug were so great that it played a practically-unknown role in the economics of the Great Rebellion. Early in the conflict, Congress authorized the president to "trade with the Confederacy when it seemed advantageous." In order to keep Billy Yank in the field, the Union urgently needed cotton. In order to keep Johnny Reb in action, the Confederacy had to have opium.

Memphis was the chief center for exchange of Confederate cotton for narcotics plus quinine and chloroform—whose supply was cut off from southern ports by the blockade. In the river city and at other points, North and South exchanged vast quantities of goods with the bargaining power of the drug-rich North rising as the war dragged on.

When hostilities ceased men who had become addicted to opium as a result of medical treatment became confirmed pill takers or "opium eaters." There were no laws governing importation or use of the drug, so the supply remained plentiful.

Many desperate victims tried patent medicines that were advertised as cures. Dr. S. B. Collins, who described himself as "the great narcologist of the age" made a fortune selling his secret but worthless "opium antidote" he claimed to have discovered in 1868.

Some addicts recovered as a result of long and painful effort. Most never mastered the drug. As a result of America's greatest wave of addiction to hard drugs, tens of thousands of Civil War veterans died still hooked upon the narcotics first administered to them through official military channels.

The founder of New Helvetia—the site of present-day Sacramento, California—was Captain John Augustus Sutter. Later he began using his first rather than his middle name.

California Land Baron John A. Sutter Lost a Fortune Instead of Gaining One When Gold Was Found at His Sawmill

A nugget no bigger than a dime started the famous California Gold Rush. It was found on January 24, 1848, by John W. Marshall. Marshall, foreman of a gang of men building a sawmill for land baron John Augustus Sutter, was an ordinary workman but his employer was one of the wealthiest men in the West.

Born in Kandern, Baden, John Sutter came to the U.S. in 1834 at age thirty-one. From St. Louis he crossed the Rockies, then wandered for four years in search of an ideal place to establish a permanent base.

He found it at the site of present-day Sacramento, in a region then held by Mexico. The Swiss emmigrant became a Mexican citizen and received a grant of about 49,000 acres on which he located his settlement of New Helvetia (New Switzerland). Sutter worked so hard to improve transportation and to build villages that he is often called "The Father of California." By the time John Marshall found that all-important nugget, Sutter held what amounted to a private kingdom that was much bigger and richer than the Ponderosa ranch of TV fame.

After the initial find Sutter went with Marshall to the millrace where the sawmill was under construction and himself picked up several tiny nuggets. "I had a signet ring made from them," he later wrote. "I had my father's trademark—a phoenix in flames- engraved on the face. On the inside was the inscription: 'First gold, discovered Jan. 1848.' Three bishop's crosiers followed, then the cross of Basle and my name: SUTTER."

That ring was practically all that John Sutter ever got from the Gold Rush.

Within days after news of Marshall's find had begun spreading, the land baron recorded in his journal: "My workers began to desert. . . . An uninterrupted procession now went past my windows. Everyone who could walk climbed the hills from San Francisco and the coastwise hamlets. As the fever swept the southern towns they too emptied. My poor domain was overrun.

"Misery now began for me. The mills ceased to work. They were plundered to the very mill stones. My tanneries were deserted. My men came to me. They implored me to go to Coloma (about 40 miles north-east of Sutter's Mill), to become a gold-seeker with them. My God! How I loathed it! But I consented at last. There was nothing else for me to do."

"I settled down to wash gold in a mountain camp on the banks of the torrent that is still called Sutter's creek," he recalled in later years. "Soon a horde of adventurers descended upon us. I struck camp and went still higher up the mountain. Useless precaution! That accursed swarm followed us everywhere.

"From the mountain top I could see the immense territory which I had cleared and fertilized given over to fire and pillage. At night the low roar of men on the march came up to us from the west, punctuated by rifle shots. At the end of the bay I watched a vast unknown city arising as though from the ground and spreading visibly each day. The bay was black with vessels."

By October, 1848, one of the interested observers was youthful

Lieutenant William Tecumseh Sherman, destined to win fame as a Civil War general. "People are arriving and departing daily and hourly," he said in a letter sent back east. "At least 400 have come from Oregon already. I have no doubt that gold in these mountains exceeds any previous calculation."

Many of the Argonauts, as gold-seekers were often called, came by wagon train. Others came from the east coast by ship in a matter of about six months. In 1849, more than 700 vessels dropped anchor in San Francisco Bay. Frequently their crews deserted and joined mobs fighting their way to the goldfields.

Inevitably, members of those mobs wrecked and then looted the empire Sutter had created. His buildings were torn down because miners needed lumber to build their shanties. His fine herds of cattle were slaughtered for food. "Shanty towns" made up of board shanties and of tents, sprang up everywhere. Sutter's life was threatened so often that he retreated to isolated Hock Farm, where he remained in virtual hiding for a number of years.

"Johann Augustus Sutter is a ruined man," he confided to his journal. "The watercourses I have made, the sites I chose so carefully for my buildings, the roads I laid out, the bridges and canals that I built are so many baits for the land-grabber and the claim-jumper. New Helvetia? Try to find it! New names are given to everything. Sutterville, Sutter's Creek, Sutter County bear the name of their old master. But these names commemorate nothing save the ruin of my establishment and the tragedy of my fate."

The rush of settlers led to California's admission into the union in 1850. Law was restored, after a fashion. But it was too late for the man who had been forced off a tract of land bigger than the canton of Basle in his native Switzerland. Sutter's domain was now occupied by tens of thousands of adventurers who filed land claims with the U.S. government.

In desperation, John Sutter went to court. Initially he sued the State of California for $25 million and the U.S. government for $50 million damages. Fought for four years, the case went to California's highest court—where Sutter's claims were declared valid. The ruling meant that San Francisco, Sacramento, and dozens of other communities stood on his private property.

News of the legal decision triggered new violence. Mobs attacked and then burned the courthouse where the decision had been rendered. Records of the case went up in smoke. The ranch to which Sutter had retreated was dynamited. His fruit trees were cut down and his cattle were shot.

New litigation brought Sutter a settlement from the State of California: a lifetime annuity of $250 per month. With no resources except that annuity he and his wife Anna took their case to Washington in 1865. California Governor Frederick F. Low, writing on October 6, 1866, said: "I earnestly commend his claims to the favorable consideration of Congress." Mark Twain, General James W. Denver, and other nationally prominent men came to Sutter's support. But "A Bill for the Relief of John A. Sutter" died in a Senate committee.

Living in a cheap boarding house, Sutter stayed in the capital in order to press his claims. April 15, 1876, saw Congress receive a sixteen-page memorial signed by General Sherman and several hundred prominent Californians. The Private Land Claims Committee of the House of Representatives recommended passage of a bill granting redress to Sutter. But this bill, and numerous later ones, failed.

On May 12, 1879, the San Francisco *Daily Alta California* ran a special editorial. Sutter was praised for opening up California, and readers were given a capsule account of his long struggle. Editors damned shysters and land grabbers who had seized his holdings, and urged Congressional action.

By then, John Augustus Sutter was past caring. Feeble and stone broke, he was in a state of deep depression.

A new bill for relief of Sutter was reported favorably by a House committee on April 8, 1880. Before the bill reached the floor of the lawmaking body the man driven from his empire by gold-seekers died a pauper, on June 18, 1880.

Sutter's Fort as it appeared in 1930

Orville Wright was at the controls for the 12-second first flight of an airplane at Kitty Hawk, N.C., December 17, 1903. He flew about 100 feet; later the same day, Wilbur covered 852 feet in 59 seconds

An Ohio Farm Boy Contracted a Lifelong Case of "Airplane Fever" While Recuperating from Typhoid

Late in July, 1896, Orville Wright came down with a fever. The family doctor examined him and pronounced it to be "a routine case of typhoid fever." Medically speaking, the diagnosis was correct. But from other perspectives it was the most mistaken diagnosis of the century—for the patient contracted "airplane fever" while recuperating.

Just fifteen years old when he became ill, Orville was already keenly interested in "nearly anything dealing with science." Like typical typhoid victims of the era, he fought for his life a few days. After his delirium passed, he remained housebound for weeks. It was during that period of enforced idleness that he and his brother Wilbur became enamored with the goal of manned flight.

Younger of five children born to Milton and Susan Wright, Wilbur and Orville very early learned to rely largely on their own resources. Their mother died while they were young. Their father, a bishop in the United Brethren Church, was often away from home for extended periods.

Lorin and Reuchlin, the two older children, had already married and left home. That meant that Katherine, the only girl in the family, had to assume the role of mother to her younger brothers. "Katherine was home from Oberlin College, on summer vacation, when I took typhoid," Orville recalled. "A trained nurse came in to help look after me when I was out of my head, but Katherine and Wilbur were my real nurses."

Each boy had his own room—just wide enough to hold a single bed plus a wash-stand and a chair. They didn't find the four years' difference in their age a barrier; almost from the time they learned to read, they read aloud to one another.

"Since I continued to be very weak even after getting over the worst of the fever, it was Wilbur who did all the reading that summer and most of the fall," Orville said. "Wilbur brought home a newspaper one day. He showed me a headline and exclaimed: 'Otto Lilienthal is dead!' "

A few months earlier, the science-oriented boys had learned a little about the noted German engineer. They knew that he had spent years studying the flight of birds, and from that study had learned how to design gliders that sometimes made wind-borne flights of considerable distance. It was on such a flight that the pioneer aeronautical engineer was killed.

Lilienthal, the Wright brothers learned from the news account of his death, was reputed to have had "more flying practice than any man alive." Yet dozens of successful flights during a period of more than five years had kept him airborne for a total of less than five hours.

Orville and Wilbur Wright talked after the older brother had finished reading the account of the accident that took Lilienthal's life. Then they fell silent for a time. Lying flat on his back in his sickbed, Orville resumed the conversation by posing a question. With the great pioneer of flight dead, who would take up his work and build—not a glider, but a flying machine?

Orville Wright at age 8; his brother, Wilbur (right) at age 13

Solemnly, the two boys concluded that they would do the job! Their decision was reached seriously, not lightly. They knew that many persons had tried to develop machines that would bear humans into the air, and that all had failed. But with "lots of time" on his hands as he recuperated, Orville believed he could use that time to find out what others had done, and perhaps devise a new approach to the problem.

When Katherine went back to college at the beginning of the fall term her youngest brother was still unable to leave the house. All that momentous fall, Wilbur read to Orville everything he could find in the Dayton Public Library about aviation. When local resources had been exhausted, the adolescents wrote to the Smithsonian Institution and asked for material about flying. They didn't then dream that they were destined to compete with Smithsonian executive Samuel Langley for the honor of being first to get an engine-powered craft into the air.

Though self-taught, the brothers were already skilled craftsmen. When they opened a bicycle shop they didn't stop with selling bikes, but learned to make all sorts of repairs and innovations. Their first biplane kite, built in August, 1899, included parts from dismembered

Bicycle shop of the Wright Brothers, behind which was the shed where they built the engine for their 1903 plane

bicycles. When Orville became the first man in history to guide a plane off the ground, the one-time invalid sat at the controls of the *Flyer*—named for bicycles he and his brother had handled back in Dayton.

After they had gained world fame, the brothers indicated in numerous interviews and talks that they never really considered whether or not they would devote their lives to science. They took that for granted from childhood. Looking back, however, they realized that they were interested in so many aspects of science that they were in danger of concentrating upon none.

It was news of the death of a noted German glider pilot, brought into a sickroom, that led the brothers to discard "a multitude of interests" and to concentrate on a single grand goal—conquest of the skies by means of powered flight. Because Wilbur outlived his brother by 36 years, he is the more widely known of the pair. But it was Orville, victim of "flying fever contracted while recuperating from typhoid fever," who was at the controls of the *Flyer* when the machine took off under its own power in December, 1903, for a maiden flight of twelve seconds and a distance of about 100 feet.

Artist's portrayal of the assassination of Garfield

America's First Primitive "Air-Conditioning System" Was Built to Help a President Fighting for His Life

On July 2, 1881, a disgruntled applicant for the post of U.S. Consul in Paris shot President James A. Garfield. En route to New England to attend commencement exercises at Williams College, Garfield was in the Baltimore and Potomac Railway Depot, Washington, when hit at close range by a .44 slug from a British "bulldog" revolver.

Instead of rushing the stricken chief executive to a hospital, aides insisted that he be taken back to the White House. He rallied briefly, then became much worse. "Send a message to 'Crete' (the pet name used for his wife Lucretia)," he said feebly. "Tell her I am seriously hurt—I am myself (rational) and hope she will come to me soon. I send my love to her.''

By the time Mrs. Garfield returned to Washington next day from a vacation trip, surgeons had arrived at a grave verdict. Dr. D. W. Bliss, the president's personal physician, headed a team of six eminent medical men. The wound was situated on Garfield's right side about four inches from the spine. Surgeons had probed with their fingers but were unable to locate the ball which they believed to have passed between the tenth and eleventh ribs.

Mrs. Garfield reached Washington about 7 a.m. on July 3 and found the capital already sweltering under the summer heat she had tried to escape by her trip. Charles J. Guiteau, the assassin, was in jail—but that did nothing to help the chief executive whose life hung in the balance. ''We simply *must* do something about this dreadful heat,'' Mrs. Garfield urged within minutes after she took her place by her husband's bed. All day she sat near his head, fanning him in a futile attempt to keep perspiration from his face and neck.

July 4, 1881, was like no other the city has ever seen—not even during the War of 1812. A contemporary observer noted that ''A few

At the wounded president's bedside

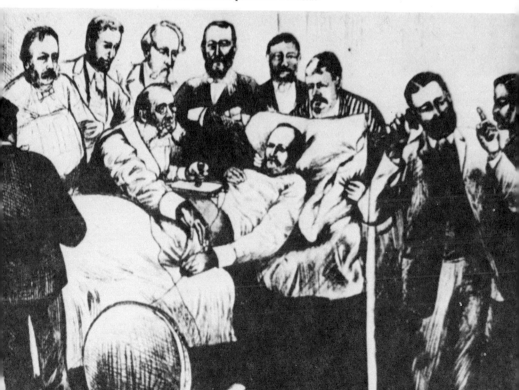

minutes before 4 o'clock the boom of a gun at the Barracks signaled the dawn of Independence Day.'' There were no parades, no speeches, no public observances of any sort in the capital. As late as 7:30 p.m. aides waiting for late news of the president's condition were dizzy from the oppressive heat.

Alexander Graham Bell was brought to the White House with the hope that he could devise a telephone-bearing circuit with which doctors might determine the position of the bullet lodged in Garfield's body. This may have been the first of all attempts at metal-finding by means of electrical equipment. Success of the experiment was, at best, qualified. Sounds picked up by the telephone did vary in pitch and intensity, but experts who listened to them were unable to decide whether they pointed to Garfield's spine, to his liver, or to his groin.

Mrs. Garfield, meanwhile, was frantic about the heat. At her insistence, doctors and their aides tried to lower it by placing ice-filled troughs of galvanized iron along the walls. Even when sheets of flannel were hung in such fashion that water from the troughs was carried upward so that evaporation would be hastened, temperature remained unbearably high.

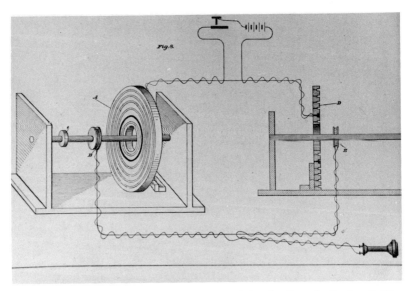

Schematic representation of one of several circuits devised by Alexander Graham Bell in a pioneer attempt to detect metal by means of the telephone —and hence to find the location of the bullet lodged in Garfield's body

At the insistence of the stricken president's wife, experts were brought in and asked to improve a crude prototype of what would now be called an air-conditioning system. A veteran mining engineer, identified only as Mr. Dorsey, was placed in charge.

"You will make available to Mr. Dorsey every article of machinery for which he may make application," said instructions to the commanding officer of the Washington Navy Yard. "You will also assign skilful and efficient engineers and machinists, with such other assistants as he may require."

Drawing heavily on his experience in moving air through mines, Dorsey secured a heavy-duty stationary engine. With it, he continuously compressed air. Heat given off as a result of this process was carried away by running water. When freed, the compressed air "became refrigerated by expansion" and absorbed heat. Before being piped into the upstairs bedroom it was forced through charcoal in order that impurities might be removed.

Hastily improvised as it was, Dorsey's system rested on basic principles still fundamental to the process of refrigeration. For its cooling effect, a contemporary machine merely uses a refrigerant gas with high capacity to conduct heat instead of the air that was employed in the attempt to save Garfield's life. According to records kept by one of the president's nurses, "by means of Mr. Dorsey's machines, the temperature of the President's room was kept at 75° or 76°." If that record is accurate, it meant that the crude "air-conditioning" equipment cut seven to twelve degrees from the peak temperature on those dreadful days in July and August.

Even so, it was obvious that Garfield was waging a losing battle. Doctors tried to improve drainage from the wound by removing a small piece of bone from a rib fractured by the bullet, but their patient's temperature remained in the range of 104°. Hoping that "sea air" might be of benefit, the dying president was sent by special train to Elberon, New Jersey. He clung to life until 10:35 p.m. on September 19, and was brought back to the capital for the most elaborate funeral since the time of Lincoln.

In the trauma of national mourning and the eagerness to see Guiteau "brought to justice," Dorsey waited for instructions but none came. On his own initiative he dismantled his pioneer air-conditioning system—compressor, fans, charcoal and all—without knowing that technological advances would have to accumulate for decades before 20th-century engineers would even attempt to duplicate his feat.

West front of Jefferson's mansion, circa 1782

Old and Broke, Thomas Jefferson Tried (But Failed) to Pay His Debts by Selling His Plantation at Lottery

In January, 1826, eighty-three-year-old Thomas Jefferson wrote to his grandson that he did not have enough cash on hand to meet obligations due local merchants for household items. Other desperate measures designed to recoup his fortunes had failed. So the ex-president persuaded the Virginia legislature to let him offer most of his land in a lottery. In spite of his great prestige, the lottery got little support—so little that when the ex-president died on Independence Day he left his family a mountain of debts.

For many years, Jefferson had owned thousands of acres of land. In 1782 only one man in Albermarle County, Virginia, owned more slaves than did Jefferson. But for most of his adult life he showed a knack for spending money faster than he made it. During his last full year as president, 1808, his out-go was almost $750 a month more than his combined income as chief executive and owner of a vast plantation.

At the end of his term as president, the founding father owned at least $8,000 on his own signature—and was obligated to pay another promissory note that he had persuaded James Madison to endorse so he could get much-needed cash.

In spite of his bleak financial outlook, the man who had drafted the Declaration of Independence never learned to restrain his spending. Captain Edmund Bacon, long-time overseer at Monticello, said that "many weeks, the twenty-six spare horse stalls were not sufficient to accommodate the mounts of visitors. I have often sent a wagon-load of hay up to the stable, and the next morning there would not be enough to make a bird's nest."

Monticello was always open to Jefferson's host of friends. Sometimes several dozen were on hand simultaneously; some stayed for weeks. Cost of playing the open-handed host drove Jefferson deeper into debt. So did his liking for fine horses and fancy rigs.

Matters became so bad that the scholarly Virginia gentleman reluctantly decided to part with one of his most prized possessions—his fine library. It was needed in Washington, where the Library of Congress had gone up in smoke during 1814 attacks upon the capital by British forces.

After the British withdrew, Thomas Jefferson wrote to his old friend Samuel Harrison Smith and authorized him to offer the Jefferson library to Congress—for a price. "I have been fifty years making it," Jefferson wrote. He did not have an exact catalogue, but was positive that it included more than 6,000 volumes—"all of them fine ones, selected with care."

Several key Congressional leaders of the era were long-time political foes of Jefferson, and were not eager to give him aid. In spite of their opposition, the lawmaking body eventually voted to accept the offer of the former president and to pay him $23,950 for books that became the nucleus of today's Library of Congress.

Even this money was not nearly enough to get Jefferson out of trouble with his creditors. As debts mounted, he continued to expand and to improve Monticello and to entertain lavishly. Eventually his unpaid obligations reached a total of more than $107,000—a staggering sum for the era.

Hoping to recoup his finances, he lay awake at night wondering what assets he could liquidate. In January, 1826, he sent his grandson Jefferson Randolph to Richmond on an urgent mission. "I have a scheme for a lottery," he confided to a few intimates. "It will injure no one, but to me it is almost a question of life and death."

In order to implement his plan, he needed a bill of authorization from the state legislature. Supporting his proposal, Thomas Jefferson wrote: "It is a common idea that games of chance are immoral. But what is chance? If we consider chance immoral, then every pursuit of human industry is immoral."

His personal dilemma, he confided in a February 17 letter to James Madison, "stemmed largely from the fact that property (land) has lost its character of being a resource. So the idea occurred to me of selling by way of lottery."

Many Virginia legislators were wary of the proposal. Jefferson's old friend, Joseph Cabell, served as a one-man lobby to work for support of a favorable bill. He recruited Dabney Carr, Jr., to assist him but the two received little encouragement. Young Jefferson Randolph ruefully reported to his grandfather that "The policy of this state has been against lotteries as immoral, and the first view of the subject was calculated to give alarm."

A few supporters of Jefferson tried to generate interest in providing from the state an $80,000 loan that would be interest-free for his life. This plan ended in talk. Finally the lower house of the legislature passed the Jefferson Lottery Bill by a margin of just four votes. In the senate, resistance collapsed a few days later.

Elaborate plans were made, and a sales organization was estab-

Still well preserved during the 1830s, Monticello was locally recognized as "America's finest private residence" (steel engraving from Dix watercolor)

JEFFERSON LOTTERY.

Register No.   Combination Nos.

1936

MANAGERS.
John Brockenborough,
Philip Norb. Nicholas,
Richard Anderson.

3 14 15

This Ticket will entitle the holder thereof to such prize as may be drawn to its numbers in the JEFFERSON LOTTERY.

Richmond, April, 1826.

           For the Managers,

Wm. Grattan, Printer.

Ticket for unsuccessful Jefferson lottery by which the ex-president proposed to place his finances in liquid state

lished with branches in big cities outside Virginia as well as throughout the state. Even though Virginia Governor John Tyler lent his personal prestige to sales rallies, the response was poor.

Two of Jefferson's old political rivals—John Randolph and John Marshall—surprised everyone by buying batches of lottery tickets. "Out of pity that the author of the Declaration of Independence has suffered public humiliation," John Randolph alone bought $500 worth of tickets.

In spite of such support, it was soon clear that the lottery would not produce enough money to pay the debts of Thomas Jefferson. Eventually the plan was abandoned. As a substitute for the lottery, without Jefferson's knowledge his friends opened "public subscriptions" for his financial relief. New Yorkers alone sent $8,500. $5,000 came from Philadelphia, $3,000 from Baltimore, and smaller sums from other cities.

Yet all efforts had failed to produce even half of the $107,000 that Jefferson owed. At his death on July 4, 1826, the third President of the U.S. left so many unpaid obligations that executors eventually sold his beloved Monticello at auction. Before the mansion became recognized as a major national shrine, nearly a century later, it had fallen into disrepair. Great care has been taken in restoring it to condition and furnishings as nearly as possible like those in the era when Jefferson ran up debts by holding open house all year around.

Today the land that Jefferson couldn't move even by means of a lottery is so valuable that a few choice acres at current prices would retire $107,000 in debts and leave a credit balance.

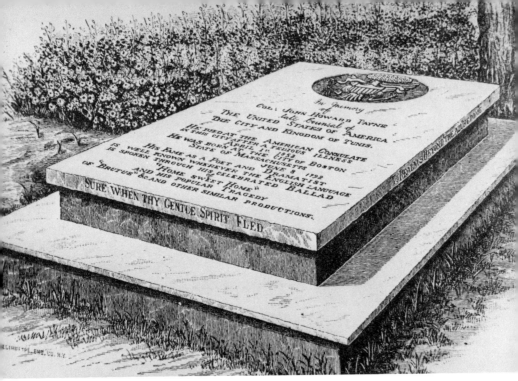

Overseas grave of John Howard Payne (inscription by R.S. Chilton, clerk, Consular Bureau, Washington)

"Home, Sweet Home" Voices the Longing of a Restless Dreamer Who Never Really Had a Home

While President and Mrs. Lincoln were in mourning for twelve-year-old Willie, who had died from typhoid fever, they invited then-famous Adeline Patti to the White House. She closed her program, then asked the Great Emancipator if he had a request. Lincoln said he had just one: "Home, Sweet Home."

Not simply in the White House in 1862, but throughout America during the second half of the 19th century, the song by John Howard Payne was high on the list of favorites. It didn't get there because the author had mellow memories of a rich and long-sustained home life.

Instead, the still-popular song is the product of a self-exiled wanderer so restless that several biographers have commented upon the fact that "even his bones did not stay still."

Born in New York in 1791 he was seldom still during childhood. His father was an unsuccessful schoolmaster who kept the family perpetually on the move. Conditions at home were so bad that at age fourteen Payne was already on his own—living in a boarding house and working as a clerk in the counting house operated by the brothers Forbes, Grant and Bennett.

Attracted to the theater he wrote—at age fifteen—a play that was performed at the Park Theater on February 7, 1806. In strangely prophetic fashion, the child playwright called his drama *Julia, or The Wanderer.* If coming things cast their shadows before them, it must have been John Howard Payne's own forty-six years of wandering that produced the theme of his first play.

Bankruptcy of his father gave him the excuse he wanted, and he made his debut as an actor on the New York stage at age eighteen—in a tragedy. For a few months he was a smash hit in both New York and Boston, but the season of 1810-11 found him without a single engagement. Plans to become a bookseller and found a literary exchange failed; at twenty he was already deeply in debt.

Friends got together a purse and he sailed for England with high hopes and empty pockets. Shuttling back and forth between London and Paris, the American became a literary hack—whose debts became larger and larger. Hoping to recoup his fortunes he leased famous Sadler's Wells Theater in order to have his own plays performed there. They flopped so badly that he landed in Fleet Street Prison as a debtor.

Bailed out once more by Henry Irving and other friends from the theater, he returned to Paris—this time, to stay. The great Charles Kemble, who thought highly of Payne, offered him £ 50 to transform *Clari, or, The Maid of Milan* into an operetta. It opened at Covent Garden on May 8, 1823, and got a thunderous ovation from a single song that was called "Home, Sweet Home." Popularity of the song didn't save the operetta, though. Even though Kemble himself was in the lead, it was played only twelve times.

Payne, still based in Paris, sometimes slipped across the English Channel to visit friends in London—and customarily used the name "J. Hayward" in order to avoid his debtors. Later, sheltered by the statute of limitations, he returned to the island kingdom and stayed there for five years. When he sailed for America on June 16, 1832, his ticket was bought with money provided by friends.

Already, his song was beginning to become a national favorite. That meant the author was something of a celebrity. Praise paid no bills and he was soon deeply in debt again—and dreaming of establishing in London a magazine for the advancement of art, science, and letters in the U.S.

In search of material for the magazine (which was never launched) he wandered into Georgia and became an early and vocal advocate of justice for the Cherokees. His efforts brought him a term in a Georgia jail on charges of being "an abolitionist, and in league with the French."

Back in New York and living on a shoestring, he finally got what seemed to be his big break. Because of his love for "Home, Sweet Home" Daniel Webster persuaded President Tyler to name the author of the song to the post of U.S. Consul at Tunis.

Upon his arrival in 1842, the new consul described his official residence in a letter. "Dreary, indeed, seemed everything," he wrote, "A YAHOO of a HOUSE, meagerly furnished, and none of the furniture mine. Not a comfortable bed in it." A partial inventory, attested by consul ad interim W. B. Gale who surrendered the property, included such items as:

> One old marble mantelpiece
> One old chandelier, incomplete
> One large flag, old and worn
> One old spyglass, with only one glass and that broken
> Six swords and five belts . . . the foregoing all damaged

Thousands of miles from the home about which he had written so forcefully, John Howard Payne, U.S. Consul, had to pay $300 back rent and then buy furniture from his salary.

Even this wretched haven was not his for long, however. President Polk recalled him in 1845—and after reaching New York he found his life "once again made wretched by creditors." Time after time he sent personal messages to Washington begging to have another chance in Tunis . . . for anything that would enable him to flee from the city of his birth.

Reappointed to Tunis in March, 1851, he lived only a few months after returning to his exile. At his death on April 9, 1856, his personal belongings were impounded for settlement of his debts. They included such items as:

Cost of a horse, $75.00
Various articles of cloth, $112.50
Freightage on a case from Marseilles, $0.80
Account of a wine merchant of Bordeaux for wines furnished in 1844, $227.50

Though it wasn't given the formal name, for practical purposes Payne was placed in a pauper's grave in St. George cemetery, Tunis. For five years the grave was unmarked. Then the U.S. government spent $91.50

John Howard Payne, from steel engraving by G.R. Hall

for a marble slab that displayed a sentimental inscription—along with incorrect dates of his birth and death.

Thirty years after the death of the homeless wanderer, wealthy W. W. Corcoran, age 85, heard the U.S. Marine Band play "Home, Sweet Home" in Washington. Corcoran arranged for bones of the author to be brought home. Disinterred in Tunis on January 5, 1883, the remains were reinterred at Oak Hill Cemetery, Georgetown, on June 9.

A contemporary observer noted—oblivious, perhaps, of the irony of his account—that "Everything possible was done to honor the memory of the man who wrote 'Home, Sweet Home,' even to the building of a special hearse, square, of plate glass, and surmounted by six urns. Practically all of official Washington was present and thousands of citizens. A monument of Carara marble had already been erected, at the top of which was a bust of Payne in later life."

Home at last, John Howard Payne would wander no more.

Steamer PHILADELPHIA, sister-ship to the ill-fated PENNSYLVANIA, and virtually identical in construction

Mark Twain's Hot Temper Cost Him His Berth on a Mississippi River Steamer—and Saved His Life

Samuel L. Clemens, destined to gain lasting fame under the pen name of Mark Twain, very early established a high goal for himself. He wanted to spend his life on the Mississippi River—in the well-paid post of pilot. Before getting that all-important license in April, 1859, he went through a long period of training.

Much of his apprenticeship was spent working as a steersman. That's the post he held on the steamer *Pennsylvania*, twin vessel to the *Philadelphia*, during most of 1858. Because Twain's hot temper flared and he quarreled with his pilot, he was put off the vessel in New

Orleans. Loss of his berth saved his life—for otherwise he would have been aboard when the *Pennsylvania* exploded and burned on June 13, 1858.

Born in the village of Florida, Missouri, in 1835, Sam Clemens moved with his family to Hannibal in 1839. He was a frail and sickly child who walked in his sleep and often ran away from home. At eighteen he left home for good in order to go to St. Louis and hunt a job. Already, he yearned to become a riverboat pilot.

Jobs proved scarce in St. Louis, so Sam set out for New York to see the Crystal Palace exhibition. That trip was the beginning of a two-year period of wandering during which he worked at odd jobs. After spending the winter of 1856 in Cincinnati he managed to get passage to New Orleans, with the idea of using that port as a jumping-off place for South America.

Horace Bixby, pilot of the steamer *Paul Jones* on which Sam travelled from Cincinnati to New Orleans, became fond of his passenger. Instead of going to South America, Bixby argued, the youth should work toward his dream of becoming a licensed river pilot. Once he got that license, he could earn $150 to $250 a month—and enjoy a position of prestige.

Clemens quickly accepted the chance to become an apprentice, responsible during training to his pilot. Up and down the river he become known as "one of Horace Bixby's cubs." Bixby, in turn, was promised a total of $500 for teaching the pilot's trade to Clemens.

By 1858 Sam had become a competent steersman. Already he had memorized many details of the approximately 1200-mile stretch of river between New Orleans and St. Louis. Still making installment payments to Bixby, he was transferred by ship owners to the sidewheeler *Pennsylvania*—and placed under the jurisdiction of her pilot.

In his famous *Life on the Mississippi,* Twain gave a vivid description of the pilot of the *Pennsylvania,* invariably designated simply as "Mr. Brown."

"He was a middle-aged, long, slim, bony, smooth-shaven, horse-faced, ignorant, stingy, malicious, snarling, fault-finding, mote-magnifying tyrant," according to Twain. "I early got the habit of coming on watch with dread in my heart. No matter how good a time I might have been having with the off-watch below, and no matter how high my spirits might be when I started aloft, my soul became lead in my body when I approached the pilot-house."

During several months that 'Horace Bixby's cub' worked as steersman under Mr. Brown, the two developed increasing mutual animosity. "The moment I was in Mr. Brown's presence, even in the darkest night, I could feel those yellow eyes upon me, and knew their owner was watching for a pretext to spit out some venom on me," Twain later wrote.

"I often wanted to kill Brown, but this would not answer. A cub had to take everything his boss gave; and we all believed that there was a United States law making it a penitentiary offense to strike or threaten a pilot who was on duty.

"However, I could *imagine* myself killing Brown; there was no law against that; and that was the thing I used always to do the moment I was abed. Instead of going over my river in my mind, as was my duty, I threw business aside for pleasure and killed Brown. I killed Brown every night for months; not in old, stale, commonplace ways, but in new and picturesque ones."

Sam Clemens managed to keep his anger bottled up inside himself until his superior officer made a savage attack upon Henry, his younger brother who had joined the ship's crew as a common laborer. After giving Henry Clemens a tongue-lashing, Brown picked up a ten-pound lump of coal and started to hit him.

"I was between," said Mark Twain, "with a heavy stool, and I hit Brown a good honest blow which stretched him out. I had committed the crime of crimes—I had lifted my hand against a pilot on duty! I supposed I was booked for the penitentiary, sure."

Though he hadn't committed a criminal offense, the youthful steersman really was in serious trouble. Brown might well prevent him from ever getting his pilot's license. That issue would have to be resolved in the future; for the moment, Brown merely ordered his subordinate out of the pilot-house and told him never to come back. Then he sent for Captain Klinefelter, master of the vessel, and demanded that Clemens be put off the ship.

In New Orleans, Klinefelter—threatened with the loss of his pilot—capitulated. He ordered Sam to "tend wharf" for a few days, then to join the crew of another vessel scheduled to follow the *Pennsylvania* upstream.

Sam Clemens protested and threatened—and then gave up his berth. He supervised loading cotton and other commodities and after 48 hours climbed aboard the *A. T. Lacey* for the voyage to St. Louis.

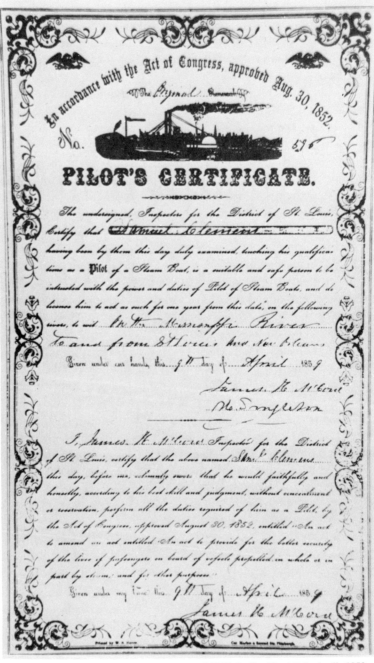

Samuel Clemens (Mark Twain) won coveted "Pilot's Certificate" in April, 1859

When the vessel reached Greenville, Mississippi, crewmen heard the dreadful news: boilers of the *Pennsylvania* had blown up on June 13, 1858, when the steamer was about four hours below Memphis.

Mr. Brown no longer posed a threat to the steersman who wanted to become a pilot; he was dead. So was Henry Clemens. So were Captain Klinefelter and 157 others aboard the ill-fated vessel.

Though it is little known to modern Americans, the explosion of the *Pennsylvania* ranks among the worst of all disasters to sidewheeler steamers. So few passengers and members of the crew survived that had steersman Sam Clemens been aboard he almost certainly would have perished. His hot temper that led him to strike his pilot saved his life and made it possible for Mark Twain to give Tom Sawyer and Huck Finn to the world.

Contemporary sketch based upon accounts of survivors shows the WEEHAWKEN going down with crew members still aboard

Bungling Seamanship Cost the Union Navy an Ironclad that Confederate Guns Failed to Sink

Engineer John Ericsson, whose innovations in naval ordnance indirectly led to an explosion barely missed by President Tyler, was the U.S. pioneer in building ironclad warships. His *Monitor*, constructed during 1861-62, gave its name to an entire class of vessels whose protective coats of metal were designed to make them invulnerable to enemy fire.

Among second-generation monitors that played dramatic roles in the Civil War was the *Weehawken*. The vessel took its name from the New Jersey town on the Hudson River that later became notorious as a dueling place. Among the many who were killed or wounded at spots close to Weehawken was Alexander Hamilton.

After a number of uneventful patrols, the monitor *Weehawken* itself engaged in one of the most furious duels of the Civil War. On Tuesday, April 7, 1863, nine ironclads under the command of Flag Officer Samuel Du Pont moved into Charleston harbor and made a frontal attack upon Fort Sumter. It was the *Weehawken* that led the flotilla.

Confederate fire from shore batteries was far heavier and more accurate than Du Pont had anticipated. An after-the-fact inquiry by naval historians established that the nine armored ships managed to get off only 154 shells—while they were targets for 2209 fired by their foes.

An observer who made an on-the-spot record of the furious battle from the perspective of Charleston's famous "Battery," or promenade ground, wrote:

"The monitor *Weehawken* led the way, pushing a raft before her to explode the (Confederate) torpedoes. Not a man was to be seen on any of the decks, and the forts were ominously silent. But when the *Weehawken* had reached the network of chains (erected in an attempt to guard the harbor), the batteries opened up all around, and she and the other monitors that came to her assistance were the target for a terrible concentric fire of bursting shells and solid bolts."

No vessel that participated in the gallant but futile operation escaped without serious damage. During forty minutes of concentrated fire, the *Weehawken* received fifty-three direct hits—two more than her sister ship *Nantucket*. Both the *Montauk* and the *Patapsco* took forty-seven Confederate shells and the *Passaic* was close behind with thirty-five.

As darkness fell Du Pont ordered his vessels into open water; naval force, alone, could never take the city in his judgment. Still, they could make life there uncomfortable. So the damaged ironclads took up patrol duty to bar merchant shipping from the port. Almost every day most or all of the vessels made a quick run toward shore, fired a few shells, and then withdrew from enemy range.

Briefly relieved of this duty, the *Weehawken* and the *Nahant* cornered the brand-new C.S.S. armored ram *Atlanta* in Wassaw Sound and overpowered her to the rejoicing of seamen, admirals, Union civilians and Abraham Lincoln. Then in an abortive September 7th assault upon Fort Moultrie the *Weehawken* ran aground between Fort

Sumter and Cummings Point. Extricated and still not crippled, the vessel was sent north for minor repairs and to have barnacles and sea grass scraped from her protective coating of iron. Minus barnacles and responding more readily to her rudder as a result, the stout ship was back in waters off Charleston by December, 1863.

A shift in assignments put James M. Duncan in command of the vessel late on the afternoon of December 5. In formal testimony he said that he had never before commanded a monitor—and that his predecessor left him no guidelines. One of the things he'd have liked to have known, Duncan told the naval board of review, was the nature and extent of his vessel's cargo.

Not knowing and perhaps finding the matter significant only in retrospect, he made a trial run that ended early Sunday morning—about the time Gen. William Tecumseh Sherman and his forces were preparing to move into Knoxville, Tenn., in order to end the siege initiated by Burnside's troops.

Charleston was enjoying one of the balmy December days for which the city is famous. With seas "almost as smooth as glass," it was natural for the new skipper to order the opening of all three hatches of his vessel so that outside air could circulate below decks. He dressed carefully, for he had been invited to lunch with Admiral John Dahlgren on the *U.S.S. Philadelphia*. Duncan climbed aboard the flagship and the gig that had brought him returned, over placid water, to the *Weehawken*.

Very early in the afternoon—witnesses gave conflicting reports of the precise time—a sudden squall hit, "coming from nowhere, out of a clear sky." Crewmen who had spent months on the *Weehawken* noticed that the vessel lurched with unusual abruptness. In the engine room, they probably talked matters over and concurred that cargo taken on the previous day was not properly stowed. After all, loading of twenty-five extra tons of coal and twenty-five tons of ammunition had been accomplished during a transition period when for practical purposes the ship had no skipper.

Whatever the precise cause of the ship's loss of her delicate balance, her movement plus the impact of a series of big waves bent heavy metal and made it impossible for crewmen to close the forward hatchway. Torrents of water poured through the one spot in her skin at which the *Weehawken* was vulnerable, since other hatches had been hastily closed.

Rescue of survivors on December 16, 1863

Below decks, a watertight bulkhead would prevent water from getting beyond the windlass room. It would take only a few minutes for pumps linked with the vessel's limber, or conduit that measured 4" by 8", to make her high and dry again. At least, that was what old hands aboard the ship expected.

But weight of the water that had gushed down the open hatch combined with weight of hastily-stored coal and ammunition was enough to tilt the *Weehawken* bow down—in such a position that powerful pumps could do nothing but suck water from the elevated stern and add to the vessel's imbalance.

Alerted by hastily-conveyed flag messages, Commander Duncan left the luncheon table and headed back toward the vessel for which he had taken responsibility just eighteen hours earlier. Before he got halfway from the *Philadelphia* to the *Weehawken* the monitor lurched again, slowly rolled to starboard, and settled in six fathoms of water. She took with her to Davy Jones' locker twenty-four valiant members of the crew, plus her log, signal book, and pay records.

In half an hour of chaos, bungling seamanship had cost the Union a badly-needed monitor that concentrated fire of heavy guns had merely battered.

Notes Scribbled on an Envelope by Self-Taught Musician Daniel Butterfield Brought Him the Only Lasting Niche He Won

Daniel Butterfield, born on October 31, 1831, in Utica, New York, was a true 19th-century American "man of all parts." He rose through the ranks to the post of major general in the U.S. Army. He built a railroad in Guatemala, later tried without success to get permission to build a trans-Siberian railroad. President of the Albany & Troy Steamboat Co., owner of the Brooklyn Annex steamships, and director of Mechanics & Traders Bank of New York, it was Butterfield whom the U.S. Postmaster General picked to study postal systems of London and Paris in 1870 in order to bring home ideas. Military forces throughout the world use the shoulder patch he originated to identify men of his Civil War unit.

Yet the versatile administrator, originator, and successful money-maker would be all but forgotten today had he not felt that he could improve on the bugle call "Extinguish Lights" that had long been the traditional final signal of the military day. At a low point in the morale of Union forces, in July, 1862, Butterfield was struck by what he considered to be the "musical pomposity" of the long-established bugle call.

"That signal is entirely too formal," he observed. "Men who are risking their lives in the name of freedom are sent to their cots by notes that resemble a trumpeting welcome to a foreign potentate. They should go to their slumber inspired to sleep well and hope for the coming of a better dawn."

98

To back up his verdict about "Extinguish Lights," the brigadier general whose troops had covered withdrawal of the Army of the Potomac to Harrison's Landing, Virginia, pulled an envelope from his pocket and quickly scribbled notes across its back. Next day he instructed brigade bugler Oliver W. Norton, of the 83rd Pennsylvania Infantry, to play the hastily-improvised call. Butterfield made a few minor changes in it, then ordered that in his brigade it should be substituted for "Extinguish Lights."

Soldiers who first heard the combination of notes said they were impressed as well as inspired. Few fighting forces of modern times have been in greater need of inspiration. Stonewall Jackson's men had humiliated Union leaders in the Shenandoah Valley. Robert E. Lee had taken the offensive against McClelland and was pushing his men away from the Confederate capital that only weeks earlier had seemed a plum ripe for the plucking. Civilian leaders in the north were already becoming weary of the war, and now it was clear that there could be no swift, easy victory.

There are many traditions about how Daniel Butterfield's new bugle call came to be known as "Taps." No such story can be documented. But abundant evidence—mostly from letters and informal diaries of fighting men—supports the verdict that "Taps" surged to popularity more rapidly than any other unpublished musical composition in history.

By the time the composer had been given command of the 5th Army Corps, on November 16, 1862, his bugle call had been adopted by one or more units in each of the Union armies. Before Christmas it was in universal use by blue-clad buglers—and in one of the strangest developments in a war filled with contradictions and paradoxes, it was by then semi-official among men in gray as well for proximity of fighting forces had enabled Confederate officers to hear the new call. Hearing it, many liked it so well that they ordered their own buglers to use it as the last signal of the day.

Many who heard and liked the hasty composition of the amateur musician didn't fully agree with his judgment about its effects. Perhaps it was intended to inspire hope for the coming dawn, but there was a peculiarly poignant—indeed, a unique—quality of what some called "muted sorrow" in the combination of bugle notes. This factor clearly fostered the quick rise and rapid spread of using the new melody for a man's "last call" as he was lowered into his grave.

Daniel Butterfield himself, by then a retired major general, experienced the special impact of "Taps" in 1888. That year, a quarter-century after the battle of Gettysburg (in which the composer of "Taps" was severely wounded), veterans of the bloody conflict gathered for a reunion. At first it seemed that survivors of those three bloody days would rear new walls of hostility between North and South.

Late in the day on July 2, as dusk approached, a bugler scrambled to a position on Little Round Top hill. From that height he played "Taps" and the notes of the universally-known melody fell on men camped along Cemetery Ridge and Seminary Ridge. Butterfield's personal reaction echoed that of multitudes of former enemies. "In a way I cannot explain," he wrote, "that bugle call by a soldier whose name I never learned wiped from my memory the last trace of bitterness carried over from the battlefields. When I reached Little Round Top I saw no blue or gray uniforms—just old comrades."

Most business exploits of the composer took place in postwar years. Successful in nearly everything he undertook, he experienced just one personal disaster. As assistant U.S. treasurer in the Grant administration he was stationed in New York—where he became entangled in the Jay Gould manipulations of the gold market that led to Black Friday, a notorious 1869 day of calamity for Wall Street and for U.S. business. Butterfield (who realized substantial profits from his ties with Gould) always maintained that he was naive rather than crooked, and the verdict of history supports his claim.

At his death in 1901 it was not the successful international businessman or even the veteran of Chancellorsville, Gettysburg, Lookout Mountain and Sherman's march to the sea . . . but the composer of "Taps" who became one of the few non-graduates to be buried at West Point.

Ellis Hughes' Big Haul Brought Him Brief Possession of the Biggest Meteorite Ever Found in the U.S.

Welshman Ellis Hughes, who had learned mining in his native country and in Australia, performed an engineering exploit so amazing that it helps to shed a bit of light on the way ancients performed such feats as the building of Stonehenge. With no motive power except his own muscles, a scrub horse and his son of fifteen, Hughes moved a 15½-ton mass of iron nearly a mile through brush and swampland.

It all started in the autumn of 1902, the year Hughes brought his family to the still-unsettled forest region that lay south of Portland, Oregon. Tired of mining and sure he'd never get ahead so long as he stuck to that kind of work, the immigrant wanted to clear a piece of land and set himself up as a farmer.

Mining was still in his blood, though, and with a partner named Dale he began scouting the nearby hills for signs of a good mineral deposit. The two men thought they had struck it rich when they stumbled across an outcropping of what seemed to be pure iron. Drawing on his Australian vocabulary, Hughes insisted that it was a fine "reef," or treasure trove whose tip had been exposed by centuries of erosion.

Cautious inquiry turned up information that the land where they made their find belonged to an absentee owner—the Oregon Iron and Steel Co. If they could borrow a few hundred dollars, they could buy the land and become rich from the high-grade iron underneath the soil.

But in order to persuade some third party to lend them money—perhaps as a partner in the venture—they'd have to demonstrate that a small investment would bring a big return.

Two weeks of digging around the reef brought bewilderment to both and frustration to Dale. Their find was not the uppermost outcropping of a huge vein. Instead it was an enormous mushroom-shaped chunk of iron that was deeply pitted and scarred. As a result of a secret assay, which showed it to be pure metal that included a considerable amount of nickel mixed with iron, the prospectors concluded—correctly—that they had stumbled across a meteorite and not a potential mine. Disgusted, Dale took off for Alaska.

Hughes pondered the situation and concluded that something could be made of their find, after all. Some time in September he decided to haul the meteorite to his own property. Once he had possession he'd set up a tent and charge 25¢ for visitors to take a look at it.

Since he had no near neighbors, Hughes attracted no attention by building a timber platform ten feet long—just big enough to accommodate the meteorite. Sections of tree trucks placed under the platform served as rollers. A homemade capstan equipped with a hundred feet of wire-braided rope and designed to be moved from one tree to another multiplied his motive power many times.

It took days of work to raise the meteorite a few inches at a time until it could be tipped on Hughes' platform. Once it was lashed in place the miner, his son of fifteen, and a scrub horse pulled on the end of the rope. Occasionally they pulled their 31,000-pound prize forward as much as eight or ten yards. Some days they struggled from sun up to sundown without moving the platform as much as its own length. On one triumphant downhill day when the ground was dry and hard they made an incredible fifty yards. By mid-November the seemingly impossible had been achieved: the meteorite lay on Hughes' land, and could now be claimed as his property and exhibited. Size of the recovered mass dictated against use of a tent, though; a shed would be more satisfactory.

Hughes had not completed his shed before trouble erupted. Executives of the Oregon Iron and Steel Co. brought legal action to gain possession of the meteorite that was, after all, found on their land. Scientist Henry A. Ward made a four-day railroad trip in order to inspect and measure the big chunk of iron and report on it for *Scientific American* magazine. He pronounced it to be a genuine meteorite and

correctly concluded it to be the largest ever found in the U.S. or
Canada. Ward underestimated the weight of the mass by one ton, but
gave it the name Willamette—which stuck permanently—from the
river that drains the region where the missile from space hit the earth
long ago.

As an outsider, the visiting scientist was struck by the almost
ludicrous prospect of a court battle designed to take from Ellis Hughes
a prize he had gained by an engineering feat that most professionals
would have dubbed impossible. "Public opinion is divided as to the
probable outcome (of the suit)," Ward told readers throughout the
western world. "But sympathy lies mainly with Hughes, the finder of
the mass and the only man recorded in common life or among scientific
collectors as having run away with a 14-ton meteorite."

Sympathy didn't sway the courts. After a brief hearing the verdict
went to the plaintiff. By now the meteorite was recognized as not
merely huge but also valuable. Hughes' attorneys appealed to the
Oregon Supreme Court and argued that the meteorite was an Indian
relic because it had been worshipped by aboriginal inhabitants of the
region. Long-established precedents made Indian relics "discarded
personal property," subject to claim by those who find them.

Attorneys for the corporation owning the land dug up a ruling from
an 1890 case in Iowa. In it, the courts had held that a meteorite is part of
the land and hence as much the property of the land's owner as a vein of
metal located beneath the surface. While this issue was still being
debated, representatives of the American Museum of Natural History,
in New York, began conversations aimed at making the institution the
legal owner of the meteorite, by purchase. As a precaution, separate
negotiations were conducted with both Ellis Hughes and the Oregon
Iron and Steel Co.

All parties to the squabble over ownership agreed to put the
Willamette meteorite on temporary exhibition so it was moved to
Portland for the Lewis and Clark Exhibition that opened on June 1,
1905. Six weeks later—on July 17—the Oregon Supreme Court dashed
all hopes of Ellis Hughes. The meteorite, said justices, had clearly
come from space—but was nevertheless part and parcel of the land on
which it fell.

Wealthy Mrs. William E. Dodge III put up purchase money to
acquire one of the most unusual pieces of "real estate" (as defined by
the court) on record. After more than a year of offers and counteroffers,

it was sold to the American Museum for $20,600. Exhibited there for years, in 1936 it was moved to the Hayden Planetarium where it is still a prized display.

Even historians who specialize in Oregon lore do not know what happened to Ellis Hughes. The man whose ingenuity and muscle-power turned the biggest of all U.S. meteorites into a legal *cause celebre* dropped out of sight during early decades of its public exhibition in the nation's largest city. The only thing he ever got from his exploit was the satisfaction of remembering he had achieved one of the most remarkable one-man engineering feats ever recorded.

Edison/Westinghouse "War of the Currents" Culminated in Sing Sing Prison

Late in the 1880s Thomas Edison and George Westinghouse were engaged in one of America's first—and most important—industrial wars. Electricity, not yet in general use, was widely considered "the energy with the greatest future." Edison had developed and was eager to market direct current equipment; Westinghouse favored alternating current and had invested everything he had in factories that would be worthless if that form of current failed to dominate the field.

In an atmosphere of high finance, industrial espionage, and rapid growth of the electrical industry its two giants brought their war to a climax on death row in Sing Sing prison.

Willie Kemmler, alias John Hart, lived in drab fashion and committed a wholly unimaginative crime by slaying his common-law wife with a hatchet. Though he never denied his guilt, when his trial began in May, 1889, newspapers of Buffalo, New York, intimated that it would be "sensational." Already there were rumors that if convicted, Kemmler might be the first man to face death by a new and untried process: electrocution. Eager for a way to make capital punishment humane, in 1888 New York lawmakers had passed an Electrical Death Act. Under its provisions any person executed after December 31 of that year would make "a fast and painless exit from the world through the power of electricity."

Language of the statute specified that *alternating current* should be used in the death house. Thomas Edison, already powerful and revered, was responsible for that clause. He and his colleagues had told lawmakers that alternating current—to which George Westinghouse had tied his future—was extremely lethal. His own system of low tension direct current, insisted the inventor, was virtually harmless— incapable of satisfactory use as a means of capital punishment.

New York State authorites, confronted with the necessity of putting together an instrument for quick and painless death by means of alternating current, knew of just one source from which to secure a dynamo. George Westinghouse himself rejected their overture. If his equipment should be used, publicity about its lethal effects could easily put him out of business.

Legislators had acted hastily and in ignorance, Westinghouse said. "The alternating current will kill, of course. So will dynamite and whisky, and lots of other things. But we have a system whereby such current can do no harm unless a man is fool enough to swallow a dynamo."

While Westinghouse balked and stalled, Edison and his cohorts went about the state staging public demonstrations designed to show the danger of alternating current. In these demonstrations, they put a number of animals to death. As yet, no word had entered standard use as a title for killing by electricity. *Scientific American* magazine noted that eighteen terms were competing for that place. Among them were: electromort; thanatelectrize, electrophony, electricide, voltacuss, fulmen—and electrocution.

Called by whatever name, the death of Willie Kemmler had to take place by means of an alternating current of electricity. That couldn't be done without the proper equipment. Since Westinghouse wouldn't supply it, perhaps his competitor would. A colleague of Edison, identified in documents of the era only as Harold P. Brown, allegedly got one of his clients in South America to order a Westinghouse dynamo. Once the machine was crated, it is said to have been re-sold two or three times in order to make it available to authorities at Sing Sing prison. There workmen began to build an electrically-wired chair whose design was already in the rough stage.

At this point the self-confessed killer received unexpected help. One of the greatest criminal lawyers of the era, W. Burke Cochran, came to the aid of Willie Kemmler. Since Kemmler clearly didn't have money enough to retain an attorney of note, it was widely believed that

Westinghouse paid the fees in order to try to halt the world's first electrocution.

All channels of appeal were exhausted. Kemmler's execution was set for August, 1890. Meanwhile, Brown had superintended completion of "the electric chair" and had tried it on animals. He told reporters that the death of the condemned man would come swiftly and painlessly because of the lethal power of the alternating current used.

He had a long list of men already accidentally killed "by running against the electric wires" he insisted. According to Brown, many of them had died from current produced by the Westinghouse dynamo—"the very machine that has been installed at Sing Sing." State Prison Superintendent Winthrop, who had followed the case closely, insisted that "death by electricity, using the alternating current, ushers in a new and humane era in the history of mankind."

Warden Durston of Sing Sing invited Dr. Carlos F. McDonald of the State Lunacy Commission to be present at the impending execution—which was to be followed by an immediate autopsy. Law officers, a justice of the state supreme court, two ministers and fourteen physicians were included among the twenty-seven witnesses permitted under New York law. All received secret messages to be on hand at daybreak on August 6.

No one—least of all Thomas Edison—dreamed that the execution of Willie Kemmler would receive more publicity and create more lasting impressions than any execution since King Louis XVI of France had died under the guillotine in 1793. For few executions have ever been so terribly botched.

Witnesses didn't have to be told when the shock of 1700 volts hit the condemned man. Pronounced dead after fifteen seconds, he soon began to sigh and struggle. There was at least one long burst of electricity after the head electrode had been strapped back in place; perhaps there were more. At any rate, current was not shut off until eight minutes after the switch was first thrown. Hair of the condemned man was singed. There was an odor of burnt flesh in the room. Numerous small blood vessels of his face had burst.

Public reaction was immediate and violent. As far away as London and Paris, newspapers condemned the "terrible torture." Experts and then members of the general public recognized that in spite of Edison's claims, alternating current couldn't possibly be lethal under all circumstances.

No one knows the total impact of that culmination of the "war of the currents" in Sing Sing. But every good biography of Edison and of Westinghouse includes references to otherwise forgotten Willie Kemmler. It took so long to kill him by means of alternating current that public support of Edison's system waned. People concluded that the Westinghouse current posed far less danger than they had been led to believe. Already, many engineers had stressed the AC-advantage of functioning with a transmission system far less costly than that for DC. Partly because of the swing in opinion that resulted from the highly-publicized first electrocution, morbid fear of alternating current vanished and it—rather than Edison's direct current—entered standard use in the U.S.

A Fugitive under Indictment for Murder Presided over the Senate Trial of Supreme Court Justice Samuel Chase

Supreme Court Justice Samuel Chase, impeached by the House of Representatives, was scheduled to be tried in February, 1805. Throughout the nation but especially in the capital, there was heated debate about the role played by Thomas Jefferson—who was eager for a conviction. As the date of the trial approached, the burning question of the day became: Who will preside?

Under ordinary circumstances that question would have been academic. But these were extraordinary times. In the election of 1800 Thomas Jefferson and Aaron Burr had received seventy-three votes each in the electoral college. Thrown into the House of Representatives in balloting that began on February 11, 1801, the contest was not decided for five days. On the thirty-sixth ballot, Jefferson was named president and Burr became vice-president. His chief Constitutional duty was that of presiding over the Senate.

There is some doubt that Aaron Burr was the perpetually-scheming totally-ambitious man depicted by some of his rivals. But he chafed in the role of vice-president, eagerly acted upon a chance to give up the post in order to occupy the New York governor's mansion—if elected chief executive of that state.

Badly beaten in the gubernatorial race, he was in no mood to tolerate attacks from his long-time rival Alexander Hamilton. Letters by three of Hamilton's friends, quoting him concerning Burr, had been made public in weeks before the election—and probably influenced its outcome. Hamilton, alleged Dr. Charles Cooper in a letter to General Philip Schuyler, had said that he regarded Burr "as a dangerous man, and one who ought not to be trusted with the reins of the government."

Sometime in June, 1804, published versions of that letter reached the vice-president. He wrote to Hamilton demanding an explanation but got what he considered an unsatisfactory reply. More exchanges of letters made things worse instead of better; Burr challenged Hamilton to meet him on the field of honor. Both men knew that a duel might lead to criminal charges—but neither would yield.

Five years earlier Burr had fought Hamilton's brother-in-law, John Barker Church, at Weehawk, New Jersey. Both men had missed with their first shot, and while the pistols were being reloaded Church had offered his opponent an apology that ended the fracas. Three years earlier Hamilton's eldest son, Philip, had been killed at Weehawk. What better place to end their enmity than on that bloody ground?

The place was settled, but not the time. It would be better, Hamilton proposed, to wait until the end of the term of the circuit court over which he was required to preside. Burr agreed. Once, on July 4, they sat next to one another at the banquet of the Society of the Cincinnati but were not observed to speak. July 11 was selected for the meeting, and both men made their wills. Samuel Bradhurst, a friend of Hamilton, tried to bring about a reconciliation—but succeeded only in prodding Burr into a duel with swords that left the Colonel with a prick in his arm.

Seconds settled upon a distance of ten paces, pistols not exceeding eleven inches in the barrel, and the determination of positions by lot. Both parties reached a ledge above the Hudson before 7 a.m. According to a document published next day by the seconds, "At the signal the fire of Colonel Burr took effect, and General Hamilton almost instantly fell." Burr was urged from the field to prevent recognition by the surgeon and bargemen who were approaching. At 2 p.m. on the following day, Hamilton died.

Burr fled to Philadelphia, lingered a few days and then accepted the invitation of Senator Pierce Butler to visit his plantation on St. Simon's Island, Georgia. Burr travelled under the name of R. King, in company with Samuel Swartwout and a slave named Peter. By now, he was a fugitive from justice.

Acting with unprecedented speed, a New York coroner's jury had on August 2 rendered a verdict of "Wilful murder." In weeks that followed, Governor Morgan Lewis and other men of influence pressed for a careful examination of the legal situation. As a result, New York dropped the murder charge for that of "challenging to a duel." Meanwhile New Jersey—on whose soil the fatal meeting had actually taken place—prepared to charge the vice-president with murder.

Burr remained in seclusion until late September, then proceeded toward Washington by leisurely stages. He reached the capital on November 4, already aware that a Bergen County, New Jersey jury had indicted him for murder. In his absence from home creditors had secured a court order under which his house and furniture had been sold to satisfy his debts.

A group of Congressional leaders drew up a round-robin petition asking Governor Bloomfield of New Jersey to quash the proceedings against Aaron Burr. Bloomfield (a friend of the fugitive) regretfully replied that under the constitution of the state, he had no power to take such action.

It was in this charged atmosphere that the nation's capital made preparation for the first trial of a Supreme Court Justice under impeachment. Few persons were neutral; they were either for Chase or against him. But with the vice-president a fugitive from the law, the city buzzed with gossip and speculation about who would preside over the trial.

Those questions were answered on February 4 when Aaron Burr took his seat in the Senate. Still under indictment for murder, he presided over the trial that brought a verdict of "Innocent" for Chase—a verdict that must have vexed Thomas Jefferson greatly. Still subject to possible extradition to New Jersey where he would have to answer for the death of Hamilton, Aaron Burr superintended the counting of electoral votes and personally handed parcels to tellers who reported a clear-cut second-term victory for Jefferson.

New Jersey authories never tried to extradite Burr, but he considered it "unwise" ever to enter the state. In New York he was disbarred and disenfranchised. Later tried for treason and acquitted, he returned to New York in 1812 and was permitted to resume the practice of law. During the last twenty-four years of his life, the man who had been among the most turbulent and controversial figures in American public life spent most of his time in his home, brooding over the past.

Samuel Langley's plane in flight, June 2, 1914

High Wind and Bad Luck Cost Samuel P. Langley the Renown Gained by the Wright Brothers

Just nine days before the Wright Brothers put their homemade *Flyer* into the air, a man with much more scientific knowledge and experience launched a machine that should have flown, but didn't. High wind and bad luck sent Samuel P. Langley's "aerodrome" spinning—and brought him ridicule instead of world fame.

Like Orville and Wilbur Wright, Langley was fascinated by science as a boy. "I cannot remember when I was not interested in astronomy," he said in later life. Born in Roxbury, Massachusetts, on August 22, 1834, he graduated from Boston High School—then

112

launched a lifelong program of self-education. He learned so readily that after a period of work as an engineer and as an architect, in 1867 he was named director of Allegheny Observatory in Pittsburgh.

Several years before leaving Allegheny in 1887 in order to join the staff of the Smithsonian Institution, the self-taught scientist became keenly interested in the possibility of flight by heavier-than-air machines. He began by building models that were powered first by "India rubber," then by steam and by gasoline.

Successful performance by several models convinced him that he was on the right track. Meanwhile, he invented and built instruments that measured the lift and drift of moving plane surfaces. His findings led him to adopt curved supporting surfaces—successfully used in a four-wing power-driven model that looked much like an oversize dragonfly. Its wingspan was fourteen feet.

Experts who later studied his detailed notes concluded that by 1894 "Langley had mastered all the basic principles of aerodynamics and knew how to build a plane that would fly." One major obstacle remained. In this era, the lightweight gasoline engine didn't exist. All power plants then in use were too heavy for an airborne machine. So the engineer-scientist built his own light engines equipped with flash-boiler steam system heated by petrol and yielding about one horsepower for each five pounds of weight.

Early in 1896 Langley's Model #5, equipped with one of his engines and catapulted from a houseboat on the Potomac, flew about 3000 feet—until the fuel supply was exhausted. In November of the same year his Model #6 covered about 4200 feet. He was now ready to build a machine that would take a man into the air.

Unlike the Wright brothers, Langley had definite ideas about the future of the machine he called "aerodrome." He knew that observation balloons had been used during the Civil War, and insisted that a flying machine—whose pattern of flight could be controlled by its pilot—would revolutionize military tactics. He knew, too, that the French government was subsidizing Clement Ader's experiments aimed at producing just such a machine as he envisioned. It would take money—lots of money by standards of the era—to finance the machine that he envisioned.

Spurred by outbreak of the Spanish-American War, a joint Army-Navy Board agreed to let Assistant Secretary of the Navy Theodore Roosevelt outline Langley's plans and hopes. Response was overwhelmingly positive. Langley was voted $50,000 for "developing, constructing, and testing a flying machine capable of bearing a man." All the money was to be poured into the experiment; Langley was to give his own time and effort gratis.

Again the problem of finding a suitable power plant became paramount. Engines used successfully in models couldn't be adapted for larger and heavier machines. Veteran mechanic Charles M. Manley, who had joined Langley's team, went with him to Europe in order to look at auto engines in use and on the drawing boards of manufacturers. Nothing they saw was precisely what they wanted.

Back in Washington, Manley started from scratch and after extensive tests and adaptations put together an engine that yielded 53 horsepower at 950 rpm. Best of all, it weighed only a trifle more than 140 pounds.

Most of the money from military sources had been exhausted. To

Samuel P. Langley—the man who almost launched the airplane age

complete his machine, Langley would have to get substantial backing from another source. It came from the Smithsonian Institution in a series of allocations that eventually came to a total of $23,000.

By 1903, Langley was sure he would get his machine into the air within the year. Complete with pilot, his aerodrome weighed slightly more than 800 pounds. With more than 1000 feet of sustaining surface and that lightweight 53 horsepower engine, the two pusher propellers would be more than adequate to give sustained and controlled flight.

July, 1903, saw the aerodrome dismantled and taken to a houseboat on the Potomac for reassembly. It was towed to a point forty miles below Washington, where the river is nearly three miles wide. But before launch day, a storm caused so much damage that the test had to be postponed for repairs. Wing ribs of the aerodrome were so badly warped that it took three months to get them back in shape. By then, winter was approaching and Langley was eager to test his machine.

Everything was ready on December 8, 1903. Again, however, the weather refused to cooperate. Very late in the afternoon tugs were brought into service to pull the houseboat so that it nosed directly into the wind. Newsmen, military observers, and a few members of Congress had assembled at Arsenal Point to see the flight.

At 4:45 p.m. pilot Charles Manley signalled for crewmen to release restraining pins so that the aerodrome would be thrown into the wind by means of a spring-driven catapult. Just as the pin was pulled, a sudden heavy gust sent the launching platform lurching. The rudder of the aerodrome—already in motion—was severely damaged. Though the machine cleared the rail, rear wings collapsed and it nosed into the water almost vertically.

That gust of wind ended Samuel P. Langley's attempts to put the aerodrome into the air. Wide publicity about his costly failure—heavily laced with ridicule—virtually obscured news that the Wright brothers successfully got their machine into the air just nine days after the disaster on the Potomac.

Until his death in 1906, Langley insisted that failure of his aerodrome stemmed from the launching process, not the machine's capacity to fly under its own power. Few persons outside a small circle of admirers took him seriously.

Eleven years after Langley failed to beat the Wright brothers into the air, Glenn H. Curtiss took the aerodrome to Lake Keuka, near Hammondsport, New York. Wary of a catapult launch because it

Langley's 1903 "aerodrome" was almost but not quite capable of flight; failure of the machine cost the inventor the support of Congressional appropriations

requires calm weather, he put "hydroaeroplane floats" under Langley's machine. Though they added more than 300 pounds, it was flown successfully on May 28, 1914, and several times later. Curtiss substituted one of his own 80-horsepower motors for Langley's and added another 400 pounds—then repeatedly flew the aerodrome "without damage to its delicate wing spars and ribs or excessive strain upon any part of the machine."

Prepared by fifteen years of scientific study of aerodynamics, backed by the U.S. military establishment and the Smithsonian Institution, and motivated by clear concepts of ways a heavier-than-air machine could become a new and decisive factor in war, Samuel P. Langley failed to become first to master the air only because of high wind and bad luck. When two rank amateurs succeeded nine days after his failure, their first acclaim came from the European rather than the American press.

Al Jolson paused in the recording of "Blue Skies" and made a 16-word comment that wasn't in the script, not knowing he was bringing the Talkies into existence.

Recorded When He Interrupted a Scheduled Song, an Ad-Lib by Al Jolson Ushered "The Talkies" into Being

Warner Brothers wanted some sort of breakthrough that would permit them to hold their lead over most competitors in the movie business. Experiments indicated that it might be possible to synchronize recorded music with movements of actors, using a newly-developed Vitaphone process. Everything else except the songs was to be in the familiar silent format, with printed subtitles for dialogue.

Once the decision to take a chance was reached, the producers started looking for a suitable story and the right actors. The story, they decided, was the 1926 George Jessel Broadway hit called "The Jazz

117

Singer.'' In it, a Jewish cantor's son turns his back on family tradition for the sake of a career in vaudeville—then comes back home on the eve of the Day of Atonement and sings ''Kol Nidre'' in the synagogue as a substitute for his father.

Technical preparation included the design and building of a soundproof camera booth—needed to prevent microphones from picking up noise made by whirring cameras.

George Jessel was offered the leading role, but turned it down. Studio representatives turned to one of the country's best-paid blackface comedians and asked him to star in a story that came close to being a stage version of his own life.

Born as Asa Yoelson in St. Petersburg, Russia, the noted entertainer was a son of a rabbi and was himself an ex-cantor. The Yoelsons came to the U.S. in 1890 as a result of pogroms of the era and settled in Washington, D.C. Asa's father clashed with the bright, headstrong boy and at age fifteen he left home to try to make a name on the stage. By the time he won a part as an extra in a Jewish epic, *Children of the Ghetto,* Asa had changed his name to Al Jolson.

That was in 1899, and he had gone straight up the ladder ever since. Already a best-seller of phonograph records, he was in a position to make his own bargain with Warner Bros.—and knew it. Producers offered him a token payment in cash plus a big chunk of stock. He indignantly turned the offer down and eventually got $25,000 on signing, plus $6,250 per week for two months. Plans called for the recording of three Jolson songs, which would be dubbed into the otherwise silent film.

Testing the recording equipment, Jolson sang ''Kol Nidre'' without an audience. Results were far beyond what he had expected. He liked the sound of his own voice so much that he frequently went to a projection room and ran the footage that included the song.

Samuel Warner supervised filming of *The Jazz Singer* on a Sunset Boulevard stage especially engineered to handle the recording of the songs. On a July day they reached a scene in which Jolson, seated at a piano, was scheduled to sing ''Blue Skies'' to Eugenie Besserer in the role of his mother.

With Vitaphone equipment in action, the man who was until then chiefly associated with blackface vaudeville put everything he had into the song. It would be a hit, and he knew it. Bubbling over with self-confidence and perhaps no longer conscious of the recording process, Jolson leaned toward Eugenie and demanded: "Did you like that, Mama? I'm glad. I'd rather please you than anybody I know of."

Once the boner was discovered, everyone on the set including Jolson, assumed that the three brief sentences he had spoken would be cut from the film. But when Samuel Warner listened to the playback he made a quick decision. Those spoken words would add to the movie, he felt, instead of detract from it. He ordered that they be retained—and script writers were put to work preparing an additional 250 words of dialogue to be interspersed throughout the movie.

Critic R. E. Sherwood of *The Silent Drama,* writing just three weeks after the October 6, 1927, premier of *The Jazz Singer* in New York, spoke for multitudes of awed moviegoers who had suddenly become listeners as well as lookers. "There is no question of doubt that the Vitaphone justifies itself in *The Jazz Singer.* It proves that talking movies are considerably more than a lively possibility: they are close to an accomplished fact. In view of the imminence of talking movies, I wonder what Clara Bow's voice will sound like . . ."

After the western premiere in Los Angeles in December, *Los Angeles Times* drama editor Edwin Schallert was even more enthusiastic. "Al Jolson's voice can now go ringing down the hallways of time," he said. "Here is a show! To miss it would be like failing to catch a glimpse of Lindbergh."

By the millions, Americans flocked to see—and to hear—*The Jazz Singer.* Too late Jolson realized that by demanding cash for his performance instead of stock, he had passed up a fortune. Transformed from a silent movie with songs into the first of the "talkies" as a result of his enthusiastic ad-lib, *The Jazz Singer* broke box-office records throughout the western world. Producers jostled with one another to get full length talking pictures ready for sound-hungry crowds. Al Jolson's refusal to take his script seriously had sounded the death knell of the silent movie.

A Song by His Son-in-Law Saved John Tyler When the Nation's Biggest Naval Gun Exploded during an Excursion

On the afternoon of February 28, 1844, President John Tyler was headed toward the deck of the gunship *Princeton*. He stopped to listen to a military ditty sung by his son-in-law William N. Waller. As a result he was not among the notables who were killed or injured in the explosion of the 10-ton cannon dubbed the *Peacemaker*.

Though the U.S. was not yet a top naval power, in 1844 national leaders were eager to challenge European nations for mastery of the seas. That would be impossible so long as American vessels were limited in their firepower to pivot guns like those used on paddlewheel steamers.

Robert Field Stockton, a career naval officer, turned his attention to the problem of building bigger and better cannon. He found that cast iron ordnance (hard and brittle) was incapable of handling shot weighing more than 32 pounds.

Stockton shifted to wrought iron. With the new material he produced in England a smoothbore cannon, the *Oregon*, that fired 216-pound balls using charges of 20 and 30 pounds of powder. Qualified success of the *Oregon* led to the forging of a second 12-inch gun—this time produced in the U.S. by Ward and Co. Preliminary tests indicated that the *Peacemaker* was substantially stronger than the *Oregon*. When both powerful guns were mounted on the frigate *Princeton* the vessel became the pride of the U.S. Navy.

Captain Stockton pulled strings, twisted arms, and managed to arrange a "gala demonstration." National leaders, including the president, agreed to take an excursion down the Potomac River in order to see for themselves the power of the great guns.

As preparation for the day, a White House levee was held on the evening of February 27. Next morning, 150 ladies and 200 gentlemen crowded aboard the *Princeton*. Cabinet members jostled with foreign diplomats, senators and congressmen, plus the elite of Washington society. No one challenged Stockton's claim that the *Peacemaker* was the world's largest naval gun—and capable, by its might, of living up to its name.

A below-deck area, converted into an impromptu salon, was the center of activity for the morning. When most guests had eaten and drunk their fill, the *Princeton* weighed anchor and began to steam downstream about 1 p.m. Dignitaries crowded the decks in order to see and to hear the *Peacemaker* fired twice. Then at 3 p.m. most of them went back below decks for the "sumptuous collation" that had been prepared as part of the celebration. President Tyler himself proposed three separate toasts—one each to the United States Navy, the *Peacemaker,* and Captain Stockton.

Many more toasts followed, then some of the guests began to sing. Someone—never identified—mounted a table and shouted a proposal that the great cannon be fired once more in order to honor "The Father of our Country whose estate we shall soon be passing." Stockton nodded agreement and hurried above deck to order the necessary preparations. Many dignitaries trickled along behind them.

President Tyler was at the foot of the ladder when his son-in-law began to sing a military ditty. Tyler felt that it would be impolite to leave until the song was finished, so waited in company of Julia Gardiner who already expected to be asked to become his bride.

As Waller reached a line that ran "Eight hundred men lay slain," a roar announced that those who had tarried would not see the *Peacemaker* fired in honor of Washington. The words of the song were so singularly appropriate that listeners burst into applause. Then an officer "blackened with powder" dashed through the gangway and shouted: "Surgeons! All surgeons! To the deck! To the deck at once!"

At the blast intended to salute George Washington's memory, the breech of the *Peacemaker* had exploded. Jagged chunks of red-hot metal sprayed over the decks had wrought incredible havoc! Secretary of State Abel P. Upshur, who had given the go-ahead for construction and arming of the *Princeton* while serving as Secretary of the Navy, was dead. So was the present Secretary of the Navy, Thomas W. Gilmer. Senator David Gardiner, father of Tyler's future wife, lay in a pool of blood—killed instantly. Senator Thomas Hart Benton wandered about in a daze, his right eardrum ruptured. Commodore Beverly Kennon, chief of construction of the U.S. Navy, was dead. So was Virgil Maxcy, President Tyler's black body-slave. Two ablebodied seamen were killed on the spot; nine received serious injuries.

Badly shaken by what he called his "narrow and singular providential escape," President Tyler noted that the watch belonging to Senator Gardiner had stopped at 4:06—while the lawmaker's spectacles were not broken.

At 4:20 the *Princeton* reached Alexandria, where the steamer *I. Johnson* took most survivors aboard. With Secretary of War William Wilkins, Tyler remained aboard the stricken vessel until 8:10 p.m. Bodies of victims were left there for the night, then taken to the East Room of the building that was still commonly designated simply as "the President's house."

James G. Birney, candidate for the presidency as leader of the Liberty Party, noted that "our fair capital has seen nothing quite like the funeral services conducted with quiet solemnity on Saturday, March 2.

"Many mourners who are political rivals of John Tyler join his admirers in wonder," said Birney, "at the marvel of the way in which a military song delivered him from imminent danger of sudden death or crippling injury."

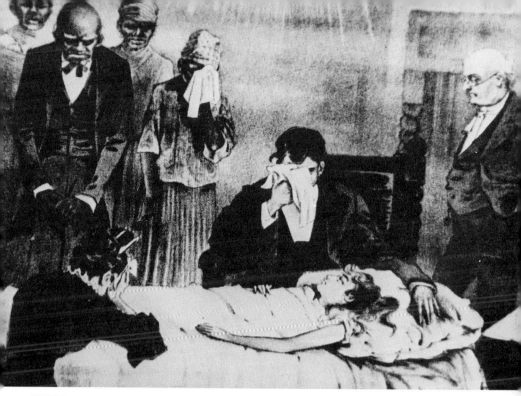

UNCLE TOM'S CABIN —detail from poster advertising production of "Stover's Great Mammoth Uncle Tom Cabin Co." —circa 1885

America's Most Successful and Influential Drama Was Taken to the Stage against the Wishes of the Author

Forty-year-old Harriet Beecher Stowe didn't have the foggiest idea of how it would affect the nation when in 1851 she began publishing a serial in the anti-slavery *National Era* of Washington, D.C. Her announced purpose was to give a faithful portrayal of everyday life among slaves in the south—about whom she had little firsthand knowledge. *Uncle Tom's Cabin; or, Life Among the Lowly,* was the end result. Practically forgotten today, the subtitle expressed the real intentions of the author.

Struggles over copyright law, brought into sharp focus during the

UNCLE TOM'S CABIN;

OR,

LIFE AMONG THE LOWLY.

BY

HARRIET BEECHER STOWE.

VOL. I.

BOSTON:
JOHN P. JEWETT & COMPANY.
CLEVELAND, OHIO:
JEWETT, PROCTOR & WORTHINGTON.
1852.

*Title page of first English edition of history-making novel whose subtitle is
now seldom remembered*

1970s by the proliferation of photocopy equipment, hadn't yet been
fought in the 1850s. Copyright of a published literary work gave the
author no rights in dramatized versions, and no control over them. So it
was purely perfunctory—a courtesy on his part—when popular singer
Asa Hutchinson requested Mrs. Stowe's permission to prepare a dramatic version of her novel that still had many weeks to run as a
newspaper serial.

Harriet Beecher Stowe flatly rejected the proposal. Many—perhaps most—of her biographers conclude that she did so on religious grounds. Daughter of Presbyterian clergyman Lyman Beecher and sister of Congregational clergyman Henry Ward Beecher, there's no doubt that she appealed to piety in her refusal.

' " . . . any attempt on the part of Christians to identify themselves with (theatrical productions) will be productive of danger to the individual character, and to the general cause," she told Hutchinson.

Did that language faithfully express the reason for her views . . . or was it a piously-worded excuse? From the perspective of more than a century, much evidence supports the latter view.

Her letters include many allusions to the theater. She was eager to know what her daughters thought about Sarah Bernhardt. She referred dispassionately to *The Black Crook*—a musical that was anathema to many church folk because of the "nakedness" it exploited. During a period spent in Florida with her daughters she joined them in sponsoring both "dancing parties" and dramatic performances. She spoke with approval about views of actresses such as Sarah Siddons and Adelaide Ristori. Gossip among the devout of Andover, Massachusetts, had it that she actually attended plays in Boston.

Vigorous, colorful, and dramatic she clearly was. Prudish by standards of the era, she clearly was not. So her refusal to sanction a theatrical version of her novel could have stemmed from fear—never publicly expressed—that dramatists and actors would somehow distort her message and destroy her characters. If that actually was the unspoken basis for her opposition to putting her story and her people on the boards, she was incredibly farsighted. Distortion began almost at once, during the 1850s, and reached a climax during the 1890s when as many as 400 to 500 troupes were devoting themselves entirely to the money-making art of "Uncle Tomming."

Harriet Beecher Stowe's original Uncle Tom was strong in his gentleness—eager not to placate his white master, but to gain entrance into the Kingdom of Heaven. Transformed under the impact of thousands of dramatic appearances by second- or third-rate actors, he became the boot-licking old man whose name entered general speech to indicate a toady willing to endure anything with the hope of saving his own skin. Bloodhounds on the ice, as handled by Jay Rial's Ideal drama group and scores of others, came to mean more to the audience than the underlying message of the novel that gave Little Eva to the world. A single glance at a playbill designed to lure listeners to the theater in order to hear Mrs. C. C. Howard sing "Oh! I'se So Wicked" gives proof positive that the Topsy of the theater was a quite different person from the Topsy of the novel.

Among dramatists, only Asa Hutchinson seems even to have asked for permission to stake a claim to the literary gold mine that was offered to the public in the form of a novel. Before final installments of *Uncle Tom* had appeared in the *National Era*, a play based on the story was being performed in Baltimore.

No dramatic version was ever sanctioned by Harriet Beecher Stowe, and she never collected a dime in royalties. But the play, complete with bloodhounds, hit the ground running and continued to gain momentum for half a century. Public clamor for it was, if possible, even greater than that for the phenomenally successful novel.

First issued in book form by J. P. Jewett of Boston in a then-ambitious edition of 10,000 copies, *Uncle Tom* sold out within a week of its appearance on March 20, 1852. By May, it had been issued in London. There was no international copyright convention to protect rights of the author, so English, German, Scottish, French, and Italian publishers pirated as they pleased. No one knows how many copies were sold. Jewett alone issued 300,000 during the first year and competitors brought out at least three times as many. By 1893 the British

Manuscript page of "Uncle Tom" (fascimile)

Museum held copies in Armenian, Bohemian, Danish, Dutch, Finnish, Flemish, French, German, Hungarian, Italian, Polish, Portugese, Greek, Russian, Spanish, Swedish, and Welsh—plus dozens of English-language editions and "versified or dramatized adaptations, extracts, and abridgements."

Proliferation of dramatized versions of *Uncle Tom* proceeded even more rapidly than that of printed ones. By 1854 New York alone saw simultaneous offerings at Purdy's National Theater, Barnum's American Museum, Christy's Minstrels, the Bowery Theater and the Franklin Museum. Each promoter tended to publicize his as "the only authentic version."

Actually, though, few promoters and few if any long-time performers made any effort to preserve the spirit and mood of Harriet Beecher Stowe's novel. Instead there was constantly jostling for "audience effect"—achieved by modification of dialogue, simplification of story line, and by putting players into stereotyped roles.

The public didn't care that pursuit of Eliza by bloodhounds was a dramatic device foreign to the novel. And in the atmosphere of national tension produced by the slavery issue, there was genuine clamor for villains who were very villainous and for heroes who were bigger-than-life by virtue of the obstacles they faced.

If bloodhounds were suddenly at a premium, so were Uncle Toms. Demand for men adept in the title role was so great that a Chicago theatrical agency dropped all other interests and specialized in finding Uncle Toms. Some of them spent most of their adult lives playing that one role. Many enlisted members of their families, who joined the cast and travelled for weeks or for years offering the public nothing except *Uncle Tom*. Simultaneously, dozens of professional "Uncle Tommers" played in London, Edinburgh, Berlin, Paris, and other cities where the Ohio River meant nothing more than a wandering line on a map of a far-off place.

Appetite for the dramatized version of "the novel that started the Civil War" diminished after the turn of the 20th century, but never vanished altogether. Mason Brothers' company, in its 57th season, was still "Uncle Tomming" in 1927. Edwin S. Porter pioneered with a movie version made for the Edison Co. in 1903; since then at least a dozen more have been put on film. Carl Laemmle's $2,500,000 version almost—but not quite—broke box-office records made by 1923 versions of *The Hunchback of Notre Dame* and *The Ten Commandments*.

As this broadside indicates, the worst fears of Harriet Beecher Stowe were realized; on stage, her epic characters were often made to appear comical.

Whether rendered by a "family troupe" stopping in Kokomo, Indiana, for a one-night stand in 1854 or by veteran actors performing before cameras, no dramatic version has been truly faithful to the novel from which it was drawn. No matter what her motives may have been, Harriet Beecher Stowe was right in withholding her name from *Uncle Tom's Cabin* in the flesh. Yet measured by any standard it is far and away the most successful and influential of American dramas. Critic-historian Edward Wagenknecht may be right in judging that, warts and all, the stage version of *Uncle Tom* "was the closest approach to folk drama that America ever made."

The SPRAY as photographed in Australian waters

Joshua Slocum, First Man to Sail Around the World Alone, Won Little Fame and Less Fortune

"Joshua Slocum is neither a hero nor a fool. He is a brilliant man made desperate because steam has robbed him of his life passion. He may seem eccentric. That is not true. He is simply passionately enamored with sailing vessels and the sea."

That verdict, delivered in the winter of 1894, should have commanded a hearing. It came from Henry M. Stanley—who had gained fame by his finding of Livingstone in Africa. Veteran New England fishermen paid absolutely no attention. Stanley, they allowed, was better qualified to speak of Africa than of the sea. From the distance of

The SPRAY sketched in a storm off New York, before Slocum left on his grand voyage

nearly a century, the summary made by Stanley appears to be surprisingly accurate.

Joshua Slocum, reared on a little farm in Nova Scotia, quit school at ten. He ran away to sea at sixteen, became captain and then owner of a series of increasingly-large vessels. In 1881 Slocum became master of the 1800-ton windjammer *Northern Light*—widely considered to be the finest sailing vessel in the world. "Steam was already cutting into the merchant trade," he recalled in later years. "I knew that when I bought my first interest in her. But I didn't expect to go broke within three years and find myself a captain without a ship."

Totally unable to reconcile himself to steam, Slocum drifted for a number of years. By 1892 he was stone broke—with nowhere to go. Then fate took a hand in his life. An old friend, Captain Eben Pierce, saw him on the waterfront and offered to give him a little vessel called the *Spray*.

Slocum hurried to Fair Haven, a few miles from Perth Amboy, New Jersey, and found the *Spray* to be a wrecked oyster boat lying on her side in a pasture. Timber by timber and plank by plank, he rebuilt the 37-foot craft during a period of thirteen months at total cash outlay of $553.62.

"She sat on the water as lightly as a flying fish ready to make its leap," Slocum said of the rejuvenated 13-ton craft after a trial run. While rebuilding her, a plan had begun to take shape. If he made some extraordinary voyage and wrote a book about it, perhaps he could recoup his fortunes.

During the winter of 1894-95, friends of fifty-one-year-old Joshua Slocum learned that he intended to take the *Spray* around the world —single-handed. Most persons dismissed the notion as a joke; a few who took it seriously gave Slocum dozens of reasons why he couldn't succeed. So few took him seriously that only the Boston *Globe* noted his April 24, 1895, departure from that port "to go 'round the world."

At Yarmouth, Nova Scotia, his logbook recorded that he took on water, kindling for his two-burner stove, salt meat, and a barrel of potatoes. Using a steering gear designed by himself, he slept with the helm lashed—and found that the vessel remained on course except when seas ran high. With favorable winds behind her, the little vessel averaged 150 miles a day.

"No one can know the pleasure of sailing free over the great oceans save those who have had the experience," he confided to his diary on the fifteenth day. By his own definition he had plenty of pleasure ahead: Yarmouth, England . . . Fayal, in the Azores . . . Gibraltar . . . and beyond.

At Gibraltar a stern British officer forbade him to proceed "because the Mediterranean is full of pirates." Slocum refused to return home, so headed back across the Atlantic by the southern route. Forty days out of Gibraltar he dropped anchor in Pernambuco, Brazil. His boom, broken in heavy seas, couldn't be repaired so he compromised by shortening it. A month later in Rio he added what he called "a jigger mast," converting the *Spray* from a sloop to a yawl. By now his announced purpose was being taken seriously; he was lionized every time he put into port.

But plaudits of men had no effect on the cruel sea. Six times he tried unsuccessfully to weather the Strait of Magellan. On the seventh try he tied himself to the helm and stayed there for thirty hours, fighting the fearful williwaws—violent squalls that sweep down from the Andes.

That was the most dangerous leg of his voyage. Compared with it the trip to Juan Fernandez Island was child's play. Slocum took special

The SPRAY leaving Sydney, Australia, equipped with new sails given to Joshua Slocum by Commodore Foy

The SPRAY moored at Fairhaven, after completing her global voyage

delight, though, in setting foot on the island where Alexander Selkirk's adventures had inspired the writing of Robinson Crusoe. After ten happy days with friendly islanders he set sail for Samoa.

This run required seventy-two days. "I saw neither smoke nor sail during the entire passage," he wrote. "Seventy-two days of absolute solitude—just the sea, the *Spray*, and me." Some of the joy evaporated when, months and thousands of miles later, he weathered a fearful storm and put in toward Newport, Rhode Island, to end his journey— only to find that the bay was mined because of the Spanish-American War.

Joshua Slocum had sailed 46,000 miles in thirty-eight months. Though his hands were bleeding when he reached home, he was in perfect health—and weighed one pound more than when he first put to sea. His book about his voyage, *Sailing Alone Around the World,* is one of the great adventure epics of all time. But it didn't make the money he had expected; it is probably more widely circulated now than when issued in 1899 by The Century Co.

Attempts to exhibit the *Spray* were unsuccessful. Even at the Pan American Exposition in Buffalo few persons were willing to pay to see the vessel. For a voyage twice as long as that which later brought world fame, big royalties, and knighthood to Francis Chichester, Joshua Slocum got nothing.

He gave less and less attention to his affairs, spent more and more time at the helm of the *Spray* with the wind in his face. On November 14, 1909, he set sail for Martha's Vineyard, outward-bound. No trace of ship or man was ever found. There's little reason to doubt that Joshua Slocum wanted it that way. Only Davy Jones' locker is a fitting resting place for the first man to circumnavigate the globe alone.

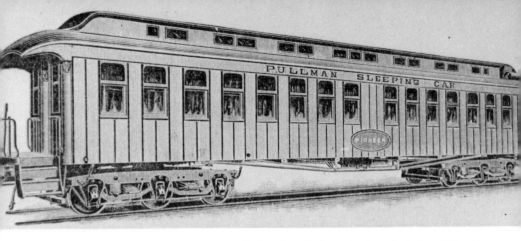

The first modern sleeping car, added to Lincoln's funeral train at the behest of his widow, was dubbed "The Pioneer"

Lincoln's Funeral Train Boosted the Pullman Car into Acceptance that Led to Dominance of the Rails

Mary Todd Lincoln passed through Chicago in an 1865 railroad journey to Springfield. Tradition has it that while waiting between trains the wife of the president was invited to take a look at the world's most elegant and expensive railroad car. She left no account of her on-the-spot impressions of the magnificent *Pioneer*—complete with Brussels carpet, many ornate mirrors, hand-carved cherry woodwork, and radically new system of berths for sleeping. Clearly, however, Mrs. Lincoln was greatly impressed by the *Pioneer* because a few months later when the train bearing the body of her martyred husband pulled out of

Chicago on the last leg of its long and mournful journey, she insisted that the *Pioneer* be attached for her personal use.

Both in Europe and in the U.S. rapid expansion of railroads had led farsighted men to experiment with cars that would permit passengers to sleep while they rode. Colonel William D'Alton Mann organized the Compagnie Internationale des Wagons-Lits to supply "boudoir cars" with compartments for four or for two passengers. T. T. Woodruff of the Terre Haute & Alton built and put into service a series of sleepers that had six sections on each side.

Former wagonmaker Webster Wagner, working for Vanderbilt's sprawling New York Central line, built cars with berths plus linen compartments for exclusive use on rails controlled by the Commodore. These and other early sleeping cars were crowded, rough, and uncomfortable. Passengers slept fully clothed and fought to hold their berths when cars lurched around sharp curves or jolted along rough sections of track.

In 1858 an ambitious young entrepreneur who had left school at age fourteen spent what he called "a comfortless night" on a sleeping car during a sixty-mile journey from Buffalo to Westfield, New York, returning for a visit to Chautauqua County where he had been born and reared. That night, George Mortimer Pullman decided that he could—

Pullman —father of the modern railway sleeping car

and would—design and build a sleeping car whose primary concern would be comfort of passengers.

Pullman was totally without car-building experience, but had a vivid imagination and plenty of nerve. Many who came in contact with him during his youth called him "brash." That title was first applied to him when, not old enough to grow a full beard, he had offered to take on a job that veteran engineers thought impossible. Widening of the Erie Canal—popularly derided as "DeWitt Clinton's Ditch"—became necessary very early in the 1850s. Owners of buildings along the margins of the ditch wanted them moved instead of torn down. Experts said it couldn't be done; young Pullman offered to try. He succeeded so well at house-moving that he built up about $6,000 in capital—enough to look for greener fields.

Chicago was ready to begin raising itself out of the swamp in which it had been built. Streets posed no major problems. But large buildings such as the Tremont hotel appeared to be doomed. Young Pullman appeared on the scene, offered to raise the four-story Tremont "without breaking a pane of glass" and got the contract. Using 5,000 jackscrews and 12,000 workmen, he made the job seem easy.

Since the Windy City was already becoming a major rail center, the New Yorker who made his money raising buildings decided to sink some of it in sleeping cars that would be more comfortable than the one he remembered so vividly. Officials of the Chicago & Alton Railroad, who had only a dozen day coaches, let Pullman convert two of them to sleepers. In them he installed hinged upper berths whose position could be altered by means of pulleys and ropes. Each car had two wood-burning stoves and passengers were provided with pillows and blankets.

Though these early cars were mildly successful, Pullman was far from satisfied with them. Six-foot ceilings made them seem cramped, and berths too short for a tall man added to this impression. It cost about $1,000 to convert each day coach and new "rattlers" built for Vanderbilt's line involved an investment of about $4,000 each. George Pullman envisioned a much bigger, much better—and far more expensive—sleeper.

By 1864 he was ready to take the plunge. With boyhood friend Ben Field as a partner, he sank a colossal $18,000 into *The Pioneer*. By far the most costly railroad car then in existence, it stood two and one-half feet higher than conventional cars and was a full foot wider. The

Interior of conventional railroad coach, built in 1865, in which passengers who traveled all night had to sleep sitting upright (Baltimore & Ohio R.R. coach)

Pioneer was equipped with hinged upper berths plus hinges that made it possible to slide the seat forward and the back down. Covered by patents # 42,182 and #49,992, these innovations produced the world's first real sleeping car—whose seats and berths could be folded for daytime travel.

So much money had been invested in the luxurious sleeper that it would never pay for itself unless passengers were charged $2.00 per night instead of the standard $1.50. Most railroad executives were wary of such high fares. And elegant as it was, *The Pioneer* couldn't be put into service. It was too wide and too tall.

In the language of railroad historian Stewart Holbrook, "the death of President Lincoln dropped into Pullman's lap a wondrous opportunity." For when the president's widow asked to use *The Pioneer* on the last leg of the journey that took the special funeral train from Washington to Springfield, officials of the Chicago & Alton got busy. Working around the clock, special crews cut platforms and widened bridges so that Pullman's wide car could squeeze by. At many points, overhead girders were raised in order to accommodate the car that towered two feet above ordinary ones.

Scheduled to leave Chicago at 9:30 p.m. on May 2, 1865, Lincoln's funeral train—with *The Pioneer* at the rear—pulled out while bells of the city were tolling. All through the night, bonfires glowed at intervals along the track. All telegraph stations were kept open continuously while crossings were guarded by crews equipped with lanterns and flags. A pilot engine ran ahead of the funeral train, keeping no less than eight and no more than twelve minutes ahead.

On that sorrowful journey *The Pioneer* made a great impression on notables aboard the funeral train. One of them, General U.S. Grant, a few months later requested and got permission to use *The Pioneer* on a journey to his home in Galena, Illinois. Again, platforms and bridges were altered—and another line was open to the luxurious sleeper destined to make "Pullman" a household word.

Propelled into the national spotlight at the whimsy of a president's widow whose every wish was honored during the time of national mourning, Pullman's huge car came to be such a symbol of luxurious travel that line after line adapted equipment to accommodate it. Slowly at first, then more and more rapidly, additional Pullman cars were built. By the end of the century they had become a standard feature of U.S. railway travel.

The dainty girl speaking firmly to Raggedy Ann may have been an idealized version of Johnny Gruelle's own daughter, for whom he created the doll
—From *Raggedy Ann Stories,* ©1918
The Bobbs-Merrill Company, Inc.

Pretending Busyness, a Bored Cartoonist Wrote Stories that Launched America's Best Loved Character Doll

Designers of the American pavilion at Canada's Expo 67 were asked to include just one typical American doll. They chose Raggedy Ann as "the classic American folk doll."

Annually, the Knickerbocker Toy Co. uses about 1,000,000 yards of cloth and 150 tons of stuffing in making the doll who emerged from pages of a book. Books about Raggedy Ann have passed the 80,000,000-copy level—topping that of any other American book for children and believed second only to *Alice in Wonderland* in the world. The Bobbs-Merrill Company, Inc., of Indianapolis, publishers of the

141

Raggedy Ann books and owner of trademark, copyright and merchandising rights to the Raggedy Ann character has licensed manufacturers to use the doll's name and face with hundreds of products that go all over the world.

All this because youthful cartoonist Johnny Gruelle worked swiftly, finished his assignments hours before quitting time, and began writing stories because fellow workers complained that he was loafing. Precisely when and where this covert activity brought a doll into being is a matter of debate. Three cities (Indianapolis, Cleveland, and New York) lay claim to Raggedy Ann along with three newspapers: The Indianapolis *Star*, the Cleveland *Press*, and the New York *Herald*.

Gruelle himself didn't set the record straight in writing before his death in Miami Springs, Florida, in 1938. But chronology of his life and accomplishments plus much circumstantial evidence gives strong support to oral traditions about activities of the young Hoosier in the capital of his state.

Johnny's father, Richard Buckner Gruelle, was a self-taught but versatile and more than merely competent artist. Because he illustrated some of the poems of his friend and close neighbor, James Whitcomb Riley, the work of the senior Gruelle gained international circulation.

Surrounded by gear and creations of an artist from infancy, Johnny never seriously considered any other vocation—but he refused to take lessons even from his father. In 1902, at age twenty-two, he landed a job as assistant cartoonist on the staff of the Indianapolis *Star*.

Long-time managing editor James A. Stuart recalled that "Johnny was one of the fastest cartoonists in the business. He would check in at 7 a.m., leaf through several papers, complete a cartoon for tomorrow's edition, and be through with his work before noon."

For a time he went home as soon as he had finished his work. But fellow employees complained so loudly that he was told to stay at his desk for a full day's work. That created a problem. He had time on his hands, and nothing to do. During this idle time Gruelle began writing— in verse—stories that he thought might amuse his daughter Marcella.

These stories, according to Indianapolis tradition, were based upon a character jointly created by father and daughter. Marcella, age eight, showed her father a faded and faceless rag doll that she said she found "in that big barrel behind the chimney in the attic." The 1910 discovery was made in the pre-Christmas season when any bright youngster is especially prone to prowl. From the place where it was

Raggedy Andy, center, is a runner-up in popularity to Raggedy Ann, right
—From *Raggedy Andy Stories,* ©1920 The Bobbs-Merrill Company, Inc.

found, the battered doll almost certainly belonged to Marcella's grandmother when she was a child.

Since the face had long ago faded away, the cartoonist used one of his brushes to give the rag doll a smile plus a nose. He attached two old buttons as eyes, then as an afterthought drew a heart on the doll's chest and beneath it lettered: "I LOVE YOU."

Marcella, enamored with her new/old doll, asked her father to name it. He suggested "Alice Benton Gruelle—after your grandmother." Marcella shook her head. Glancing about for inspiration, the man who made his living by drawing political cartoons picked up a James Whitcomb Riley volume illustrated by his father.

The sketch that accompanied Riley's poem about the raggedy man caught his eye, but he couldn't resist turning to his own favorite which depicted the "orphant" to whom Riley gave no name but Annie. Abruptly the two components merged; there was just one proper name for Marcella's ragged waif: Raggedy Ann.

Originally used only in his own daughter's play, it was this doll that became the central character in stories Johnny Gruelle penned during idle hours at his desk. He moved to Cleveland and continued to write about Raggedy Ann for the amusement of the family. While there he entered a New York *Herald* contest for gag cartoonists. More than 400 of the 500 entries were eliminated, then judges reduced contenders until only two were left. When the envelopes with the artists' names were opened, Gruelle was found to have drawn both final entries. That's how he made the transition from Cleveland to New York.

While on the *Herald* payroll for the purpose of designing and laying out a new comic page, "Mr. Twee Deedle," he learned that a widely-read comic strip can often become the basis for a book. "Mr. Twee Deedle," was less than a smashing success. So Grueel turned back to old manuscripts and changed his Raggedy Ann stories into prose rather than verse. Illustrated by his own sketches, the stories were a hit from the day of publication in 1918. Raggedy Ann—later joined by her brother Raggedy Andy—remained the central character throughout more than forty books. Translation of those books has introduced Raggedy Ann to children of the world who speak more than 150 different languages.

James Whitcomb Riley, Hoosier philosopher-poet of the homespun variety, was intellectual godfather to Raggedy Ann. By a strange set of circumstances, his impact upon imaginary characters who are very real to children didn't stop with her. Harold Gray, another Indianapolis *Star* cartoonist, was particularly impressed by Riley's poem about "Little Orphant Annie"—from whom Gruelle's doll gained half of her name. Moving from Indianapolis to Chicago as a staff artist for the Chicago *Tribune*, Gray used the set of verses by Riley as inspiration for the comic strip "Little Orphan Annie."

The Great Dynamite Conspiracy

The Accused Labor Leaders, the Man Who Accuses Them and the Scene of the Outrages That Shocked a Continent

W. J. BURNS DETECTIVE (AT LEFT), J. J. McNAMARA, PRISONER (AT RIGHT), AND McNAMARA'S HOME IN CINCINNATI, O.

Photos above a June, 1911, news story showed Burns, left, with boyish-looking labor leader McNamara who claimed he was merely a target for anti-labor capitalists

Dynamite Explosions in Now-Forgotten Labor Wars Propelled Private Detective William J. Burns into World Fame

From early 1905 to late 1910, sixteen U.S. states were gripped in a now-forgotten labor war over the issue of the closed shop. At least eighty-six explosions took place during the period. Railroad bridges were destroyed or damaged. Big stockpiles of structural material were made useless. With dynamite and nitroglycerin, the standard explosives of the era, losses ran into many millions of dollars. Labor-management tensions mounted because many union leaders insisted that owners were deliberately destroying their own plants in order to make labor look bad, while owners pressed for the arrest and conviction of labor leaders whom they blamed for the wave of destruction.

On October 1, 1910, the three-story building of the Los Angeles *Times*—published by bitterly anti-labor Harrison Gray Otis—exploded and then crumbled. Few of the nearly one hundred men working the early-morning shift escaped without injury; twenty of them died on the spot or in hospitals to which they were taken. Otis borrowed presses to issue a one-sheet extra devoted exclusively to the wholly unsupported charge that "UNIONIST BOMB WRECKS THE 'TIMES' ".

In the fever heat of public reaction, Los Angeles Mayor George B. Alexander departed from accepted procedures. At taxpayers' expense he retained private detective William J. Burns to enter the case in cooperation with the San Francisco Police Department.

Born in Baltimore in 1861 and reared in Ohio, Burns had become a detective purely by chance. When his father became police commissioner of Columbus, Ohio, William saw an opportunity to pick up some extra money by helping authorities solve mysterious crimes. That led him into investigation of election frauds and then into the U.S. Secret Service. In 1909 he left the federal payroll in order to join William P. Sheridan in forming the Burns & Sheridan Detective Agency, with headquarters in Chicago. Sheridan sold out the following year, so the always-flambouyant Burns changed the name of his organization to the William J. Burns National Detective Agency.

In that era there were no TV shows to extoll the prowess and virtues of the private eye. Many who accepted cases without the authority of a badge to support them ran afoul of the law. Ordinary citizens tended to rank private detectives with, or at most just one cut above professional criminals. Burns was called into the San Francisco case largely because he had broken an important case there while still a member of the Secret Service.

When he accepted the case he had no idea that it would become a *cause celebre* in the organized labor movement. Nor did he dream that it would generate a steady flow of page-one news for fifteen months, frequent headlines for another three years, and cause the nation's most prominent criminal lawyer to promise never again to plead a case in California.

From the start, it was clear that the destruction of the *Times* building was deliberate rather than accidental. But the devastation was so great that techniques of the era were not sufficiently refined to enable investigators to find fragments of the bomb. The case might have been closed as an unsolved mystery had not strage suitcases been delivered on the morning of the explosion to the homes of publisher Otis and the secretary of the Merchants and Manufacturers Association—roughly equivalent to today's Chamber of Commerce. One suitcase exploded when detectives tried to open it, but the other yielded dynamite of the type used in quarry work plus a cheap alarm clock and a network of wires.

Burns had investigated an apparently unrelated bombing in Peoria, Illinois, just three weeks before the *Times* blew up. In the Illinois case there was property damage to the steel firm of McClintock, Marshall & Co., but no loss of life. Burns and his men were puzzled, though, at the coincidence by which the same type of high-grade dynamite had been used in both instances. Clearly, too, a skilled professional had been involved in Illinois as well as in California. Unreliable fulminating caps were then in general use. But both at the steel works and the newspaper plant it appeared that dynamiters had used a direct electrical spark activated by some sort of timekeeping device.

A break in the Peoria case led Burns to Ortie McManigal of Indianapolis, Indiana. He, in turn, led the detective to "J. B. Bryce"—who turned out to be James B. McNamara. In itself, identification of McNamara was not significant. But the suspect was the younger brother of the Indianapolis-based International Association of Bridge and Structural Iron Workers. Iron workers were noted for their activity in strike-breaking—and a disproportionate number of unsolved dynamitings had involved steel mills, steel bridges, and buildings in which steel girders were employed.

By late April Burns had a mass of circumstantial evidence plus McManigal's promise to give state's evidence with the hope of getting a light sentence. (Plea bargaining, in the contemporary sense, hadn't yet become an accepted practice.) McManigal's testimony, alone, seemed adequate to secure convictions. Burns moved so swiftly that he himself probably disregarded the law more than once, but late in April he arrested John McNamara in Detroit.

Arrest of the union leader made headlines in Europe as well as throughout the U.S.—and triggered a wave of support for the accused man. Longtime A. F. of L. president Samuel Gompers launched and quickly completed a drive to raise a defense fund of $300,000. Clarence

Strongly pro-McNamara crowds waiting to glimpse labor leaders on December 1, 1911, did not know that on that day they had entered pleas of guilty.

Darrow was retained to defend the brothers McNamara. A hastily-produced and emotion-charged movie, which pictured the labor leaders and associates as victims of a conspiracy, was exhibited wherever organized labor was strong. Darrow argued that the arrest and extradition of John McNamara were extra-legal, and persuaded an Indianapolis grand jury to indict Burns on a kidnapping charge.

In this climate practically everyone including Burns expected an early acquittal when jury selection began in October, 1911. There was no doubt about public sentiment in Los Angeles. Pro-McNamara banners, buttons, and newspaper editorials generated a great deal of enthusiasm. Anarchists—known to have a liking for San Francisco—were generally felt to have been responsible for the dynamiting of the *Times*.

At the advice of Clarence Darrow, on December 5 the accused men entered pleas of guilty. "Work of William J. Burns," said Assistant District Attorney Joe Ford, "drove them to confession as a means of escaping the extreme penalty." Clarence Darrow was twice indicted on separate charges of bribing jurors; when he promised never to plead another case in California the matter was dropped. Intermittently in the headlines for another three and one-half years, the story of violence came to an end when all men who had a part in the *Times* dynamiting were found and convicted.

By then, "William J. Burns" was virtually synonymous with "private detective." In the process of gaining international fame the detective who had voluntarily surrendered his badge brought respectability to a vocation suddenly made glamorous.

"Occident," owned by Leland Stanford; trotting at a 2.30 gait over the Sacramento track, in July, 1877
—A Muybridge photo copyrighted in 1877

Development of Motion Pictures Was Triggered by Wealthy Horse-Lover Leland Stanford

Leland Stanford won fame as governor of California, builder of the Central Pacific Railroad, and United States senator. Persons who knew him intimately agreed that more than any of those roles he liked that of breeder and trainer and racer of fine horses.

Most persons who spent time around stables and race tracks were interested only in an animal's bloodline and speed. Stanford, who had studied law and had no formal training in anatomy, was absorbed with the problem of how a horse runs. He called the movement "poetry in motion," but was unable to decide whether an animal moves at high speed by pulling with his forefeet or by pushing with his hind feet.

A long-established and widely circulated tradition, unsupported by documentary evidence but wholly plausible, holds that Stanford got

151

into a dicussion of the matter with James R. Keene and Frederick MacCrellish. Stanford, according to this tradition, ventured to suggest that "at some point in his gait, a trotter may actually have all four feet off the ground." Keene and MacCrellish are said to have scoffed so loudly at this preposterous notion that the railroad president offered to wager $25,000 that he was right—and was promptly taken on by the two doubters.

Regardless of whether or not that is the precise genesis of Stanford's otherwise hard to explain goal, he set out to prove himself correct by means of cameras. Hints and brief references in his letters and public statements indicate that he had fixed upon the idea as early as 1870. In order to test the camera's capacity to show how a horse runs, he needed an expert photographer.

Such a person reached California in 1872. Eadweard J. Muybridge, who had gained his experience and made his reputation in England, was one of the most noted photographers of the era. He agreed to try to see if he could get a shot of a horse with all four feet off the ground.

Photography was in its infancy, however, and no known equipment was capable of making an exposure in less than one-twelfth of a second. That time interval was much too great to freeze a racehorse in action. But in a period of only five years, equipment was developed that permitted an exposure of just one one-thousandth of a second. Muybridge had that equipment when he returned to California in 1877.

Leland Stanford's Palo Alto farm, located at the site of present-day Stanford University, had a fast track plus a promising stallion named Occident. It took only a few days for Muybridge to produce a still shot that baffled many veteran horsemen who shook their heads in disbelief when they saw Occident flying through the air with all four feet uplifted.

Not satisfied with having won his argument or his bet or both, Leland Stanford persuaded the English photographer to try to get photos showing every position in a horse's stride. It took a year and at least $40,000 to get all the equipment ready.

Early attempts to trip cameras by means of strings stretched across the race track failed. Stanford brought in John D. Isaacs, an amateur photographer and professional designer of railroads. Isaacs scrapped the use of strings designed to activate cameras when struck by a horse's leg, and went to what was ultra-sophisticated equipment for the era.

He placed a series of cameras at precise intervals along the track, then linked each with a cylinder equipped with pins arranged in spiral fashion. Elaborate electrical circuits made it possible for revolution of the cylinder to activate each camera in precise succession—one after another. Trial and error revealed that when cameras were properly spaced it was possible to get a dozen different photos of Occident during a single stride.

Not until many sequential sets of photos had been snapped did anyone involved in the experiment think of projecting such stills in rapid succession. Here it was clearly Muybridge the photographer and not Stanford the horse lover who conceived and executed the idea. Early in the fall of 1879 Muybridge gave a demonstration to guests who had come to the Stanford mansion. They exclaimed in awe as equipment whirred, twenty-four separate photos of Occident followed one another in rapid succession—and the horse appeared to be running.

Stanford's biographer, Norman E. Tutorow, terms that exhibition "the world's first home movie." It was, in fact, the first time in human experience that anyone—amateur or professional—had conveyed the impression of rapid movement by means of quick-moving still photos arranged in sequence for that purpose.

Leland Stanford footed the bill for publication of a then-expensive ($10) volume, chiefly photographic, about *The Horse in Motion*. Edited by J. D. B. Stillman, M.D., whose interest centered in the physiological aspects of racing, it evoked a suit for damages by Muybridge. He lost the case but the book did not sell. Most copies were purchased by Stanford, stored in his San Francisco mansion, and destroyed in the fire of 1906.

Though the book was a commercial failure, it had a profound impact. Muybridge became a sought-after notable on the international lecture circuit—expected, of course, to show a few seconds of Occident's running by means of what the photographer called his "zoogyroscope."

In Europe and in America scientists and inventors set out to transform the zoogyroscope from a toy into a new tool with which to feed visual information to viewers. One of those most interested was Thomas Alva Edison. He made important contributions to the developing art, others added their refinements and innovations, and the motion picture came into being. Edison's interest was so keen that he actually produced talking motion pictures, of a sort, about 1913—more than a

Many Muybridge photos —not just one —showed Leland Stanford's racer with all four feet off the ground simultaneously. (Sequence here is not identical with that of Muybridge's original photos)

decade before an unplanned variation from a Warner Bros. script produced the first commercial talkie.

Not even tradition gives any hint as to whether or not Leland Stanford ever collected $25,000 from James R. Keene and Frederick MacCrellish. But every careful survey of the birth and infancy of motion pictures includes at least a footnote acknowledging that the curiosity of a wealthy horse lover triggered their development.

The originator of Monopoly, once broke, made from it enough money to handle real currency almost as casually as big-denomination "play money" he used in the game.

Dreaming of "Making It Big in Real Estate," an Unemployed Salesman Developed Most Successful High Finance Game

Charles B. Darrow, of Germantown, Pennsylvania, was one of millions who could find no work during the Great Depression. In spite of the fact that he was drawing no paycheck, he urged friends and neighbors "Never dream a little dream!" In keeping with that point of view he mused about ways to make a fortune in high finance—and developed a game that became an outlet for his fantasies. The game became "Monopoly," avidly played nearly everywhere in the world except in the U.S.S.R. where it is banned as "a decadent instrument of capitalism."

"Esther, my wife, worked with me on the game," he said after it became a perennial best-seller on the list of famous Parker Brothers Co. "Few people had jobs then; many spent their time fretting. Esther and I wanted something more constructive with which to occupy ourselves."

Born in Cumberland, Maryland, in 1889, Darrow was educated at the Phillips Brooks private school. He worked as a sales representative for several makers of power plant equipment, then moved into the home heating field. As sales manager for I. W. Stearns Co. in eastern Pennsylvania he pushed "the Coppus Blower," a device designed to burn small (and hence cheap) sizes of anthracite coal in domestic

Avid European players of Monopoly use boards that display street names of their own cities—such as Paris

(Copyright 1935, 1946, 1961, Parker Brothers, Inc.; used by permission)

furnaces. It couldn't compete with then-inexpensive fuel oil, though, and sales trickled to a halt.

"We were hard pressed to make ends meet," Darrow later said. "I about that time devised a contract bridge score pad that gave the players the proper hand valuations, the bids and responses—all in a concise form for ready reference.

"I also made up jigsaw puzzles and did any odd jobs to keep the wolf from the door. I experimented with a beach bat (a toy with bat and ball for play on the beach) but it was far from a success."

Some time in 1930 the man willing to work at any odd job that came along began to fantacize. Atlantic City, New Jersey, a long-time vacation spot where money flowed freely, seemed to him an ideal spot where a man with a small amount of capital could use it to build a fortune by trading first in real estate, then in banks and railroads. Soon he devised a table game based on his dreams of easy money.

"The original product was most primitive," Darrow recalled. "The board was hand drawn on a circular piece of linoleum, colored with samples of paint acquired at any paint store. Title cards were typed on cardboard, and the houses and hotels were cut out of beading picked up at the local lumber yard. We made the game for our own amusement alone, and at that time had no thought of selling it."

Asked in 1957 to put his recollections of the origin of "Monopoly" on paper, Darrow continued: "When we tried the game out with our friends, almost invariably the winner seemed to want a copy—and the runner-up was convinced he would win next time, and also frequently ordered a game.

"Having nothing better to do I was quite willing to make up a copy for which I charged $4. One or two sets a day was the limit of my production ability. Sales quickly passed production. So after making a hundred or more it became imperative that I seek other methods.

"A friend of mine, F. Lyton Patterson of the Patterson and White printing company, offered to print up the boards—still on oilcloth—plus the title cards and other straight printing, leaving the assembly and other details to me. On this basis I could handle about six games a day . . . and again sales overtook production."

Darrow entered into a contract with Patterson and White for a complete printing, packing, and delivery job. Toy departments of local stores became interested, and the idea spread from Philadelphia to other cities. "I never spent a nickel for advertising," said the inventor

Unlike Europeans, Japanese players of Monopoly wheel and deal in Atlantic City real estate —complete with Japanese subtitles.
(Copyright 1935, 1946, Parker Brothers, Inc.; used by permission)

of the game. "It was just word-of-mouth; I'd get a letter from Biloxi, Mississippi, or Los Angeles—'send me a dozen games.' "

By the time Darrow had personally retailed an estimated 17,000 sets of "Monopoly," he realized that it was getting too big for him to handle. He wrote to "two of the important game people," both of whom told him that the game was not desirable because they didn't think they could make any money from it.

Darrow continued to handle the game personally, in lots of 1000 to 3000 sets. Then a representative of Parker Brothers Co. contacted him—because "they were getting a lot of competition from the 'Monopoly thing,' as they called it."

In 1935 the developer of the high finance game sold out to the world's largest manufacturer of table games. Eventually "Monopoly" spread throughout the developed world. Numerous versions in languages other than English have been developed. Most Europeans prefer game boards on which streets of their own capital cities are substituted for street names from Atlantic City. Japanese players of "Monopoly" retain Atlantic City street names—with miniature subtitles in their own language.

After his game became world famous, the inventor visited Atlantic City—in order to receive from the mayor the key to the city. The key-giving ceremony was staged at Park Place and the boardwalk—and Park Place was then renamed Monopoly Square.

Royalties earned from sale of more than 70,000,000 sets enabled Darrow and his wife to retire to a 37-acre Ottsville, Pennsylvania, estate. From it they travelled all over the world.

Nearly everywhere we went we found people playing "Monopoly," said the once-broke salesman who put his own big dreams on linoleum and cardboard. According to his analysis, success of the game is a result of the fact that it is "a game based on life itself; a game of commerce. It imitates the world around us; railroad, hotels, houses and utilities are very real things in both life and 'Monopoly.' Even in 1932, some of the persons who began dabbling with my play money actually had jobs!"

"Monopoly" is universally known; its creator is practically unknown. Had he been able to pay his rent on the modest home occupied in 1929, he might never have had that country estate or those trips around the world. For the most successful of all games about business and finance is the product of a man who withdrew in imagination into the world of Atlantic City because he simply couldn't face life without fantasy.

Even his most ardent admirers labeled Sylvester Graham as "exceedingly intense"—in actions as well as in appearance

Temperance Crusader Sylvester Graham Left Just One Lasting Memorial: the Cracker that Bears His Name

Enthusiasm for "natural foods" and for "health foods," perhaps at an all-time U.S. peak during the 1970s, crested briefly nearly a century and a half earlier. One man, more zealous than logical, sparked a brief but significant early craze. He didn't have any scientific basis for his arguments, but unknowingly anticipated by decades the findings of nutritionists.

Sylvester Graham was born on July 5, 1794, as the youngest child of seventy-two-year-old clergyman John Graham—who had studied at Yale fifty-four years before Sylvester made his debut. The elder

Graham survived the trauma of becoming a father at age seventy-two only two years. How much, if any, the circumstances of his birth affected young Graham remains a matter for conjecture.

This much, however, is a matter of record. After working as a farmhand, clerk, and itinerant teacher he decided that there must be a better way to make a living. At age twenty-nine he entered Amherst Academy with the intention of preparing himself to take up his dead father's mantle. Formal training was brief; faculty members labelled Graham a "stage actor" and made a formal notation of their decision that they "were disinclined to permit him to proceed with his studies."

Some men thrown out of school after one term would have gone back to the farm; Sylvester was made of sterner stuff. Presumably without the benefit of ordination, by 1831 he was "stated supply" serving a Presbyterian church at Berkshire Valley in Morris County, New Jersey. By then he had already found his real niche in life—the temperance movement.

As general agent for the Pennsylvania Temperance Society he went on the road for a six-month lecture tour. Simultaneously he embarked on a self-directed crash-course of study. Physiology, diet, and regimen occupied most of his attention. Presbyterians of Berkshire Valley, New Jersey, would have to look elsewhere for pastoral care.

At least as early as 1832, Graham had developed an elaborate program that was at first designed primarily to help drunkards push their bottles away. Temperance, he insisted, would stem naturally from sensible but Spartan health practices. Hard mattresses, cold shower baths, open bedroom windows, pure drinking water and daily exercise were essential. Most important of all, proclaimed the self-appointed prophet, was the use of coarsely ground unbolted flour.

Americans, then as now perennially poised to adopt almost any well-publicized fad, flocked to Graham's support. In many of the larger eastern cities, Graham boarding houses sprang up. A few Graham health resorts were established, and many Graham Societies offered free lectures to the public while requiring members to take strict vows concerning diet and daily habits. Little was said about the use of ardent spirits; it wasn't necessary. Practically speaking, Sylvester Graham was right—any person who followed his Spartan regimen was likely to find whisky less and less appealing.

There is no record that brewers attempted to strike back. But bakers did in at least one instance. Protesting Sylvester Graham's insistence upon use of "his" flour, Boston bakers nearly rioted when he spoke at Amory Hall in the winter of 1837. Since the mayor confessed that he was unable to maintain order, ardent Grahamites barricaded the lecture hall then placed members of a shovel brigade (armed with slaked lime) on the roof of the building where they could dump the stuff on attackers.

Harpers' New Monthly Magazine considered the incident of sufficient magnitude to deserve special treatment in an 1880 article about "The Isms of Forty Years Ago." Long before that, Emerson had castigated Sylvester Graham as "the poet of bran bread and pumpkins." That didn't prevent prominent persons as well as common folk from flocking to Graham lectures. At least intermittently, the great Horace Greeley was a practicing Grahmite.

Collapse of the movement was less dramatic than its meteoric rise, but still it came swiftly. Graham's *Treatise on Bread and Bread-Making* (1837) and his two-volume *Lectures on the Science of Human Life* (1839) were not enough to prop up his already-tottering edifice. Publication of the *Graham Journal of Health and Longevity* was abandoned in 1839 and the once-spectacular celebrity in the field of hygiene began to give Bible lectures.

According to the *Dictionary of American Biography*, there was more than a touch of pathos at his death in 1851. He gave up the ghost "after submitting to stimulants (!), a dose of Congress water, and a tepid (not a cold!) bath."

By then, the U.S. no longer boasted even one Graham boarding house or health resort. Most of the societies he had organized were already disbanded. But great numbers of persons who had eaten bread made with Graham flour either liked the taste and texture or believed firmly that it was more nutritious than bread made with conventional flour.

Millers who had at first ground Graham flour with reluctance had so many calls for it that some began to specialize in producing it. Persons who had briefly renounced pork, tobacco, salt, stimulants, and feather beds (condemned by Graham as conducive to unchastity) retained their liking for Graham bread even when they went back to their old intemperate ways.

Just as popularity of Graham bread began to wane some housewife or commercial baker decided to put the unbolted flour to new use. Who first did it and where is an unsolved riddle. But Graham crackers gained a bigger and longer lasting group of followers than Graham bread claimed even in its heyday. There is no known printed use of the term "Graham cracker" before 1882—but by then the new product of the oven was so firmly established that it not only maintained its foothold in the U.S. but was beginning to gain acceptance elsewhere.

Today the name of Sylvester Graham is a commonplace part of the vocabulary of persons throughout the western world, so much a part of everyday speech that capitalization is commonly dropped. Wherever it is baked and crunched, the graham cracker perpetuates the memory of a theatrical crusader for temperance whose ideas about processing wheat into flour long antedated the scientific findings that pronounce him to have been right.

Radio's First Entertainer Was a 14-Year-Old Kentucky Farm Boy

Professor Reginald A. Fessenden of the University of Pittsburgh is usually credited with having given the world's first radio program. His broadcast of December 24, 1906, took place at Brant Rock, Massachusetts, and consisted of a violin solo plus a brief speech, a poem, and a request to report on the quality of reception. Fessenden used a 40 h.p. steam engine linked with a 429-foot antenna whose outside diameter was 36 inches.

Almost four years earlier, on New Year's Day, 1902, fourteen-year-old Bernard Stubblefield gave an audience of about one thousand persons a brief but varied program. Stationed at the transmitter of a set built by his father, young Stubblefield talked, whistled, played the harmonica, and counted slowly from one to twenty-five. Five listening stations—one of them a full six blocks distant—had been set up about the Calloway County Courthouse square in Murray, Kentucky. Persons gathered about those listening stations stared at one another in awed silence as Bernard's voice came through.

A correspondent for the *St. Louis Post-Dispatch*, who probably exaggerated, wrote that "Simultaneously everyone at the receivers heard him with remarkable distinctness. At that moment, Stubblefield became a prophet with honor in his own country."

Entertainment by the boy was merely a device to test equipment built by eccentric genius Nathan Bedford Stubblefield—who seldom gets so much as a footnote in scholarly volumes about the beginnings of radio. His only monument of consequence stands on the Murray State University campus and hails him as "the father of radio."

Born in 1859, Stubblefield didn't complete grade school but very early developed a passionate interest in electricity. His lifelong absorption with it, plus his fear of being cheated out of his discoveries, caused neighbors to regard him as "queer." Small wonder. In an era when adolescent boys were almost as interested in fast horses as in pretty girls, young Stubblefield spent all of his spare time in the office of the county newspaper, reading back issues of *Scientific American* magazine.

Somewhere—probably in pages of the learned journal he learned a little about the discoveries of German scientist Heinrich Hertz. It was Hertz who demonstrated, about 1886, that energy can be transmitted in the form of electromagnetic (or "hertzian") waves. If a person could learn how to control those waves, reasoned self-taught Nathan Stubblefield, he could reproduce sounds at a distance. That would make possible the development of a wireless telephone system.

Alexander Graham Bell had come very close to discovering what we now call "radio" as early as 1877. If Nathan Stubblefield read the *Scientific American* for May 24, 1902, he probably snorted with impatience. For the magazine that appeared nearly eighteen months after he had publicly demonstrated apparatus with which to transmit and receive sounds without use of wires described Bell's failure to realize what he had found.

"Prof. Bell was experimenting to ascertain how slight a ground connection could be had with the telephone," said a feature article by Waldon Fawcett. "Two pokers had been driven into the ground about fifty feet apart, and to these were attached two wires leading to an ordinary telephone receiver. Upon placing his ear to the receiver, Prof. Bell was surprised to hear quite distinctly the ticking . . . of the electrical timepiece at Cambridge University, the ground wire of which penetrated the earth at a point more than half a mile distant."

Bell never came close to realizing that he could transmit sounds by means of electrical waves that were not conducted by wires. Stubblefield, labelled "an electrical engineer" in that same issue of *Scientific American,* grasped the significance of the phenomena that

Bell didn't regard as important. It was this leap of intuition on the part of a Kentucky farmer that caused him to give most of his life to work on his "wireless telephone."

Stubblefield's first crude equipment was finished in 1882. He gave a demonstration in the courthouse square—and people agreed that it was "something different," but let the inventor know they thought he was wasting his time. Ten years later he tried improved equipment in a private test. "Hello, Rainey! . . . Hello, Rainey!" came through clearly as he addressed Dr. Rainey Wells, later to gain regional fame as founder of Murray State University.

Wells tried to persuade his friend to patent the "vibrating telephone" that needed no wires, but the farmer-inventor feared he'd lose his secrets if drawings and descriptions were sent to Washington. Even in 1902 when Nathan put his son Bernard at the transmitter in order to give townsfolk the world's first public demonstration of speech and music designed to entertain and to persuade by means of electrical waves, there were no patents.

Success of the hometown demonstration was so great that Stubblefield and his son went to Washington. There on March 20, 1902, with Bernard again transmitting, they gave what the Louisville, Kentucky, *Courier-Journal* of the following day described as "A practical test of wireless telephony over a distance of a third of a mile." The "program" was practically the same as that earlier aired back in Kentucky: brief spoken messages, harmonica music, and counting aloud.

May brought a third demonstration—this time in Fairmont Park, Philadelphia. Using slightly refined equipment, Bernard's voice was "clearly heard a full mile from the transmitter." That demonstration took place just two weeks after Nathan had belatedly secured patent #887,357.

Convinced that his "wireless telephone" would make him rich, Stubblefield needed money to promote it. He got it by giving up his patent and his equipment in return for 500,000 shares of stock in the newly-formed Wireless Company of America. Too late, he learned that shrewd promoters had formed the company—which failed in 1903—as a device to get control of his invention. He got U.S. and Canadian patents on an improved transmitter but never made money from it. Modified only a trifle, in Canada it sold years later for $7,500,000.

Long before that deal took place in the burgeoning field of radio, the Stubblefields—father and son—had accepted their defeat. Nathan became a recluse, living in a cabin he built from split trees buried in the ground—and roofed with corn shucks. Cheated and ridiculed, he died of malnutrition in 1928.

Bernard and other survivors took their claims, as heirs of the inventor of radio, to the courts. Eventually the U.S. Supreme Court ruled in their favor—but by then the statue of limitations had run out and Nathan Stubblefield's patents were in the public domain. Sophisticated equipment devised by Lee De Forest had long ago supplanted Stubblefield's crude but workable system. So only that monument at Murray State University and brief notices in newspapers of 1902 preserve the memory of the first public entertainment by means of what later came to be called radio.

Veteran banker William C. Ralston, who staked his reputation on "the great American diamond find," committed suicide when the fraud toppled his financial empire.

Two Backwoodsmen Hoodwinked Tiffany's in America's Most Elaborate Version of "The Pigeon Drop"

Throughout the western world, police are continually at work trying to protect citizens and recovering money lost through one or another form of "the pigeon drop." Written references to this confidence game first appeared in 1817 when *Niles' Register* described the case of William Kennedy who was fined and sent to prison "for cheating in a game, called in the indictment, *'High cockneyrorum, or drop-the-pidgeon!'* "

The "pigeon" dropped as bait for a victim is usually a pocketbook, envelope supposedly stuffed with currency, or a packet of negotiable securities. Confidence men, working in pairs, offer to share the "pigeon" . . . for a price. Motivated by greed, the victim puts up money and discovers, too late, that the "pigeon" is worthless. Senior citizens with little business experience are the usual victims. In America's most elaborate version of the con game a pair of backwoodsmen deceived Charles Tiffany plus his gem experts—and gulled San Francisco's most prominent banker of a fortune.

Philip Arnold conceived his plan while working as a bookkeeper for the Diamond Drilling Co. in San Francisco during the 1860s. The 1866 discovery of the Kimberley fields in South Africa had stirred world interest in gems previously believed to be concentrated in India.

Children of a Boer farmer had picked up "a pretty pebble" from sand along a bank of the Vaal River. Their mother gave the pebble to a neighbor—who took it to an expert and found it to be a diamond worth $2,500. Though no one then knew that stones taken from the Kimberley fields would eventually exceed $1 billion in value, speculators throughout the world were highly susceptible to diamond fever. The next big strike might come practically anywhere.

Geologists hadn't yet determined the characteristics of formations likely to yield diamonds—and except for a small circle of European lapidaries, few persons in the world except diamond miners had ever seen uncut stones. This climate of eagerness plus ignorance meant that there were some fat pigeons waiting to be plucked. Logically, that should have been done by well-informed crooks with connections in Amsterdam or London. Defying the laws of probability, the job was pulled off, instead, by Philip Arnold and his accomplice John Slack.

Bearded, unwashed, and weary from months of prospecting, the two men appeared in a San Francisco saloon on February 2, 1872. Arnold toted a canvas sack as they sampled the drinks in one saloon after another. Always, John Slack was at his elbow with a Winchester held at the ready. Both men repeatedly turned away questions, refused to say what that all-important sack held. After two weeks they became weary of lugging their sack around and—insisting on strict secrecy—deposited it in vaults of the Bank of California. From his years as bookkeeper in the bay city, Arnold knew that bank president William C. Ralston had already made a fortune—and intended to multiply it.

The "drop" proceeded exactly as Arnold had hoped. A teller examined the contents of the canvas sack, then hurried to tell Ralston that "a couple of tough-looking miners have left a fortune in jewels for safekeeping.'' Ralston could hardly believe his eyes when he opened the sack to confirm the fact that it really did hold recently-mined diamonds sprinkled with a few raw sapphires and rubies.

Instead of approaching their prospective victim, Arnold and Slack waited for him to take the initiative. Ralston made discreet inquiries about the pair and learned that Arnold had been a member of Morgan's Raiders during the Civil War. A military connection would be helpful, the banker decided. So he recruited former Army general George D. Roberts to strike up an acquaintance with the men whose strike seemed to have potential for making the Gold Rush seem like a very small thing, indeed.

Arnold appeared to be suspicious of Roberts, but eventually warmed up to him. With his partner, he had indeed found diamonds, he said. But a full-scale mining operation would take big money that he couldn't raise without selling the sack of gems already discovered. Such a sale would start a stampede, Arnold feared, and he'd never get his share of the gems.

Roberts persuaded Arnold that "a handful of men of the right stripe—men who will want their share, but aren't so greedy that they will cut you out" could finance the large-scale operation that was obviously required. Of course, it would be necessary to proceed discreetly. Grateful for the kindness of a distinguished community leader, Arnold allowed as how he was really relieved. It was he who suggested that "you ought to get an expert to take a look at the stones"—and who stipulated that the location of the diamond field must be kept secret until land could be acquired.

San Francisco jewelers examined gems that had been brought to the city in a dirty canvas sack, and assayed them at about $125,000. That was good, but not quite good enough for Bill Ralston who had been quietly lining up investors in case the venture should take shape. At his suggestion about one-tenth of the stones were taken to New York—where Charles Tiffany had agreed to take a personal look.

The head of America's most distinguished jewelry firm confirmed the verdict that diamonds dug up "somewhere in Arizona" were of immense value. He was reluctant to give an appraisal, so called in his own lapidaries and instructed them to spend at least two days examining and weighing the gems. On the basis of their report, Tiffany told William C. Ralson that when cut the diamonds would bring at least $150,000. If the entire cache proved of equal quality, it would mean that

Arnold and Slack had for two weeks dragged a canvas sack holding $1,500,000 worth of stones from one saloon to another before deciding to store them in a safe place.

Ralston, who had made careful preparation, acted swiftly; it was vital to do so in order to gain a monopoly on American-mined diamonds. His newly-organized San Francisco and New York Mining and Commercial Co. soon had $2,000,000 capital with which to work—and was besieged by eager investors. So many inquiries poured in from Europe that Ralston somewhat reluctantly agreed to place Auguste Gansel, an agent of Baron Rothschild, on the board of directors of the company.

Arnold confessed to Ralston that he realized the enterprise was getting too big and too complicated for him to comprehend. So he sold out for $600,000. John Slack got a small fraction of that total; Arnold took the bulk of it, retired to Elizabethtown, Kentucky, and set himself up in business as a banker.

In September (less than eight months after Arnold and Slack had first made their appearance in San Francisco saloons) geologist Clarence King located the site of "America's only diamond mine" and quickly proved it to have been salted. Arnold had spent more than a year in Holland in order to buy, a few at a time, substandard uncut stones worth not more than $25,000.

A California grand jury held that Arnold had engineered one of the most audacious swindles on record and asked that he be put on trial. Kentucky authorities—who may have taken secret pride in the fact that a backwoodsman had proved himself smarter than rich Yankees—refused extradition. Arnold eventually surrendered $150,000 of his loot in return for immunity from prosecution. He lived quietly as a rich small-town banker until he became involved in a brawl with a competitor and was shot dead in the street in front of his bank.

Bill Ralston reimbursed other investors in the company from which he had expected to make a fabulous fortune. His already top-heavy financial empire collapsed and less than two years after the great diamond fraud was exposed his body was found floating in San Francisco bay.

Mrs. Winchester's house grew so vast that when it is seen from above it appears to be a complex made up of numerous separate houses.

Guided Only by Ghosts, Sarah Winchester Spent $5,000,000 and 38 Years in Constructing America's Strangest Mansion

Sarah Pardee, the belle of New Haven, Conn., society during the late 1850s, had received every possible advantage that money could buy. She was an accomplished musician, knew four languages, and had been carefully schooled in use of clothing and jewelry. In an era when daintiness was much admired, she had the advantage of weighing less than one hundred pounds and measuring well under five feet even when she wore high French heels.

William Wirt Winchester fell madly in love with her a few months before or after she turned twenty. (She's known to have been born in late September or early October, but never bothered to record the date—probably 1839.) Winchester's father, Oliver, had perfected the famous Winchester rifle and was well on his way to making one of America's great early fortunes.

Sarah married William on September 30, 1862, and ordinary working folk who heard or read about the high-society wedding were sure that the couple "had everything." At first it seemed that the verdict was correct. But their only child, Annie Pardee Winchester, survived just 39 days (3 times 13) after her birth on June 15, 1866.

By then, Civil War sale of rifles had boosted the family fortune to a level that made the name Winchester one with which to reckon in financial circles—as well as in frontier forays. Never robust, William's health deteriorated. Eventually he was found to have tuberculosis. In spite of receiving the best medical treatment money could buy, he died on March 7, 1881.

Forty-one-year-old Sarah was left without a husband, without a

No fairy castle, the house Mrs. Winchester built was (for her) a potent instrument to ward off evil.

Roof lines, steeples, and other architectural features were made deliberately complex so that it would require longer to complete them.

child, but with an estimated $20,000,000 plus 48.8% of stock in the Winchester Repeating Arms Co. Stock alone brought her about $1,000 a day—tax free until 1913. That sounded as though she was next door to heaven . . . until the lonely and broken-hearted woman began to wonder how many ghosts had been created by the rifles from which her fortune came.

Strongly-established tradition holds that she paid several visits to a Boston medium, seeking advice. There are no documents to support this account; all of her life, Sarah Winchester was so secretive that she even tried to keep her niece and secretary, Margaret Merriam, in the dark about what they were doing and why. Medium or no medium, this much is clear: in the aftermath of her husband's death the wealthy widow concluded that so long as the sounds of construction were heard in her home she wouldn't be bothered by evil spirits.

She abruptly cut most of her early ties and settled on then-isolated Los Gatos Road in the region destined to become San Jose, California.

Located on 192 acres of land, her 6-room ranch house was a good nucleus around which to form a sprawling mansion designed to fit her personal wants alone.

Today, the house whose continuous construction stopped only at her death in September, 1922, has about 160 rooms (an exact count cannot be made, because it's debatable whether or not some structures are actually rooms). There are about 10,000 windows and precisely 467 doorways along with 47 fireplaces, 52 skylights, 40 staircases, and one bell tower.

The most widely accepted explanation for the strangest one-woman building craze on record traces it to advice given by that anonymous Boston medium. Mrs. Winchester was told, it is said, that so long as sounds of hammers and saws were heard she would not be troubled by spirits of Indians or frontier bullies or Confederate soldiers felled by slugs from Winchester rifles.

Within weeks after relocating in California, the lonely and fearful woman had completed a blue Seance Room. For years she retired into

Regal in her coach, a life-size figure of Mrs. Winchester helps visitors to grasp the enormous contrast between the small woman and the vast house she built.

it for a period every night, in order to receive architectural advice from
friendly ghosts—the kind who do no harm, and who have no more use
for evil spirits than do humans.

Guided by her ghosts, by 1906 Mrs. Winchester and her crew of
12-30 carpenters had thrown up a monstrous 7-story castle with too
many rooms to count. Earthquake damage that year was so extensive
that she left the still-unfinished mansion and spent about six months
on a houseboat ("The Ark") moored in the bay at Redwood City.

Advisors from the spirit world admonished the woman who was
doing her best to please them. Instead of building up, they told her, she
should expand horizontally. As a result her mansion was trimmed to
four stories in height—and over a period of thirty-eight years when
work continued even on Christmas Day it sprawled and protruded and
twisted with no apparent purpose except that of keeping hammers and
saws at work.

Visitors who look at a stairway that leads nowhere or who lean
forward to peer through a window that has no outside opening may be
looking at remnants of earlier days. For Sarah Winchester kept a

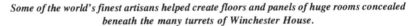

*Some of the world's finest artisans helped create floors and panels of huge rooms concealed
beneath the many turrets of Winchester House.*

What is the function of stairs that lead nowhere? They provide work for carpenters, so that the sounds of hammers and saws never quite subside.

separate crew of workmen tearing down completed turrets, balconies, porches, towers, chimneys and entire rooms. Most persons who entered her employ stayed for 15 to 20 years; one carpenter remained on the staff for 28 years. These long-time veterans of the mysterious house said that Mrs. Winchester probably constructed about 750 rooms—each personally designed by her with the expert advice of friendly ghosts.

A widespread tradition holds that Winchester House was always in the process of building in order to keep all disembodied spirits away from the place. Not so. Even an amateur ghost-hunter knows that while evil spirits avoid contact with the number 13, it fails to dampen the ardor of friendly spirits whose intentions are good. Winchester House has 13 bathrooms; many closets have 13 coat hooks; chandeliers hold 13 candles; rooms are equipped with 13 windows.

Mirrors discourage spirits—even good ones—because they become frightened when they fail to see their shadows. A person wanting to keep all spirits out of a house would be likely to install a big mirror on every wall of every room. Sarah Winchester did nothing of the sort. Her colossal architectural monument was equipped with just two mirrors—one in her favorite bedroom, another in an adjoining bath.

These factors and many more point to the conclusion that the woman who inherited the fortune made by the gun that won the West was eager to discourage evil spirits—but equally eager to make the place comfortable for friendly ones. It was from her ghostly advisors, consulted in the Seance Room, that she learned what features should be emphasized in construction and what features should be minimized or eliminated.

Germany, Poland, Yugoslavia, Italy, Belgium, England, Ireland, and other Old-World nations have their famous haunted castles. Nothing on the other side of the Atlantic even begins to compare with Winchester House—designed with the dual purpose of frightening and confusing evil spirits while making friendly ones feel at home.

Totally inadequate for a dwelling place of more than a few humans in spite of its $5,000,000 construction cost when labor and materials were cheap, the house created by Sarah Winchester with the help of her unseen advisors is now a California Historical Landmark that daily attracts hordes of curious humans . . . and no one knows how many friendly ghosts.

In later life, once-impoverished Phips wore fine clothing and lived in "a lordly manner."

The 21st Child of Poor Settlers Was the First American to Retrieve a Vast Treasure Trove from the Sea

With the development of sophisticated electronic devices plus new kinds of diving gear, treasure hunting has become an exotic and big-time international pursuit. Few successful 20th-century treasure hunters have realized so much financial gain as did a colonist born in a rough cabin on the Maine frontier in 1650. No contemporary seeker of treasure from the sea is likely to match the fashion in which William Phips rose from the status of twenty-first child of poor settlers to that of first royal governor of Massachusetts—with a title conferred by the king of England.

Adventurers of many nations had long known that great wealth lay somewhere in waters off Spanish Hispaniola, the island now including the Dominican Republic and Haiti. Probably but not positively during the fall of 1642, a fleet had passed through these waters on the way to Spain. Most or all vessels transported treasure; that commanded by the vice admiral had been sitting low in the water under the weight of precious metal looted by conquistadors from palaces, temples, and royal treasuries of South America.

It was one thing to know that silver and gold lay there for the taking, quite another thing to discover and retrieve the precious stuff. Expeditions were costly, and could be undertaken only with the backing of rich speculators. Tradition held that the Spanish galleon had struck a reef—but in these waters, there were reefs galore. Many stretched for miles, and the water was too deep to locate the sunken vessel from the surface of the sea.

Numerous adventurers, mostly English and mostly men with long-established connections, made futile attempts to find and retrieve the Hispaniola Treasure. Captain Edward Stanley, an officer of the Royal Navy operating under a commission from King Charles II, stayed at the task longer than most. He devoted three years to the search, returned home empty-handed after having spent a small fortune provided by his backers.

In the climate of gloom created by Stanley's return to England, a brash American colonist reached the island kingdom. William Phips had boosted his fortunes by taking as wife "the propertied widow of John Hull." More to the point, he had gained experience as a treasure hunter by finding and raising portions of two vessels whose only fault was that they held little gold or silver.

Under English law defined in 1276 by the statute *de officio coronatoris* and never seriously challenged, treasure trove belonged to the Crown. But in order to claim it, a ruler must get his hands upon it. It had therefore long been customary for the king to grant a charter to a treasure hunter, reserving a portion of it (often as much as half) for the national treasury.

Phips' proposal to find the Hispaniola treasure for which Stanley had searched three years in vain was by any standard a long shot. Therefore His Majesty graciously settled for ten percent of whatever his servant might find. Phips' chief backer was Christopher Monck, second Duke of Albermarle. Along with a company of noblemen and merchants, Albemarle got together nearly £4,000. That was enough to buy the 200-ton *James and Mary* plus the 50-ton frigate *Henry of London* and equip them with a diving tub plus salvage instruments.

A royal warrant of July 18, 1686, authorized Phips to recover and return to England "all flotsam, jetsam, lagan, bullion, plate, gold, silver, coin, bars or pigs of silver, ingots of gold, and other goods shipwrecked and lost before July 16, 1689, on the north side of Hispaniola." For his pains the leader of the expedition would get one-sixteenth of whatever he might find.

For more than sixty days after he and his men reached the vicinity of the region he proposed to search, Phips did nothing more exciting than butcher pigs so their flesh could be "jerked" and careen his ships in order to grease them with tallow. In January, 1787, Phips' divers began searching the banks—but had no better luck than did those who worked for Stanley month after fruitless month.

Late on the afternoon of January 17 an empty-handed diver returning to his ship by means of a small boat noticed an unusually fine specimen of coral. Vine-shaped leaves, veined in red, made the "sea feather" a prized (but not a valuable) consolation prize. He jumped into the water to seize it—and was dumfounded to find several huge naval guns lying on the floor of the reef.

The sea feather led William Phips to the Hispaniola treasure, which for forty-five years had eluded all who searched for it. Coral had covered so much of the Spanish vessel that both the prow and stern were hidden from sight, even under water. But presence of the guns was enough to warrant slow movement of the *James and Mary* and the *Henry* into position—rapid action would have tipped off rivals who were keeping an eye on the expedition.

Anchored a mile or more from the reef, the mother ships sent out small boats for the actual recovery job. For six weeks following the dropping of anchors on February 16, seamen helped Phips' four experienced divers operate their primitive "tub." The flow of gold and silver from the ocean's bottom was interrupted only on Sundays—reserved for rest and for worship. February 26, a typical good day, yielded "small Dollrs 11,009; halfe Dollrs 1,700; and a quantity of broaken Plate." A bad day in early March yielded only 3,931 Spanish dollars ("pieces of eight") plus 1,500 half dollars.

In mid-April, alarmed by rumors that a French privateer had entered nearby waters, Phips ordered his vessels home—knowing that he left behind at least half of the treasure. His arrival in the Thames during the first week of June set off a nationwide wave of jubilation. Delivered to the Comptroller of the Mint by the Commissioners of the Customs, the Hispaniola treasure was solemnly and carefully weighed.

The formal certificate showed that untaught William Phips had retrieved 37,538 pounds of pieces of eight; 25,556 pounds of bars and cakes; 347 pounds of plate; and 25 pounds 7 ounces of gold. Total value of the haul was in excess of £200,000—at least $20,000,000 in terms of today's purchasing power.

For his daring and his ingenuity—and his luck—Phips got £12,000 in cash. Then he was invited to Windsor Castle in order to be knighted at the hand of King James II. The one-time ship's carpenter returned to the New World as wealthy Sir James Phips—destined to rise to high military rank before being named royal governor of Massachusetts in 1692.

His friend and colleague Cotton Mather wrote a long and rambling life of William Phips that was published first in London and later in the colonies. This account of accomplishments by America's first discoverer of vast underwater treasure includes no reference to that all-important sea feather—whose role is reported in ships' logs plus journals of crew members.

Irish-Born William Paterson Triggered Creation of the U.S. Senate—and a Congressional Double Dividend for New Jersey

Born in County Antrim, Ireland, late in 1745, William Paterson was just five feet two inches tall and described as weighing just 120 pounds when "soaking wet." What he lacked in size the diminutive college-trained lawyer made up in tenacity. As an influential delegate to the Federal (or "Constitutional") Convention that determined the structure of the U.S. government, Paterson was outvoted when he presented a plan merely to modify the Articles of Confederation. But the "great compromise" triggered by that plan led to creation of the U.S. Senate and—eventually—to grossly disproportionate influence of New Jersey in Congress.

Delegates—seventy-four of them—had been named to convene in Philadelphia in the spring of 1787. Only fifty-four of them ever reached the City of Brotherly Love; when they set out from home only a handful (perhaps one in ten) expected the convention to frame a document such as the Constitution that eventually emerged from their debate.

From the beginning, it was clear that several issues would split the convention down the middle and that one—representation by states in a federal law-making body—might well prevent the establishment of a lasting union among former British colonies.

A handful of big and wealthy states, feared representatives of small and poor states, were likely to become all-powerful. If that was not the goal of the Virginia Resolves presented by the Commonwealth's Governor Edmund Randolph, it clearly would have been the effect of adoption of those resolutions. For Virginia (backed by Pennsylvania and by Massachusetts) boldly proposed a national legislature of two houses. According to the plan, the lower house would be elected by the people on the basis of state population—and the upper house would be selected by the lower. Adoption of the plan would have had the effect of placing the reins of government in the hands of lawmakers elected from the three big states.

Delegates debated the Virginia Resolves for four hot and increasingly acrimonious weeks. Acting as a committee of the whole, the convention voted on June 11 to establish proportional representation for the upper as well as the lower house of the legislative body that was to be created. It looked as though the influence of small states would be very small, indeed.

But when the convention reassembled on June 14 diminutive William Paterson, speaking with great fervor, requested adjournment until the next day. The delay, he explained, would enable the completion of a "purely federal" plan of government. When presented to delegates on the 15th it proved to be a revision of the Articles of Confederation under which every state, however small, retained much of its sovereignty.

Even the most ardent advocates of a system that would "prevent small states from being enslaved by large ones" privately conceded that the Paterson Plan never had a chance. But it might have the effect of blocking adoption of the Randolph Plan drawn up by the Virginia bloc—and forcing dissolution of the convention without any decisive action.

Referred to the committee of the whole, the diametrically-opposed plans were debated to the point of weariness and frustration. Finally, on July 16, Roger Sherman of Connecticut rose to propose a plan that became famous as "the great compromise." Let state representation in the lower house of Congress be determined by population, he suggested. But in the upper house permit the smallest state to be equal to the largest by giving every state two senators.

James Wilson of Pennsylvania had spoken against the Paterson Plan with great fervor. "Shall New Jersey have the same right or council in the nation with Pennsylvania?" he demanded. "I say no! It is unjust—I never will confederate on this plan!" Paterson, equally firm, had put himself on record for all time: "I will never consent to the present system (the Virginia Resolves, as amended by the committee of the whole), and I shall make all the interest against it in the state which I represent that I can. Myself or my state will never submit to tyranny or despotism!"

Spokesmen for opposing plans—largely but not entirely influenced by the size of states from which they came—grudgingly conceded that Sherman's compromise seemed to offer some satisfaction to both factions. Under it, heavily populated states would dominate the House of Representatives—designed to have a decisive voice in taxation and other fiscal matters. But a Senate made up of two persons from each state would preserve the essential feature of the Paterson Plan— namely, "a legislative chamber in which the states would vote equally, without regard to population or wealth."

As a governmental structure, the Congress of the United States actually was something new under the sun. Large states could make their influence felt, but would be powerless against a coalition of senators from small states. But the requirement for joint approval of bills would mean that no band of senators pushing for special interests of small states could overpower the House of Representatives whose numbers would be determined on the basis of proportional representation.

Expediency and a mutual desire to achieve some sort of compromise, not legislative brilliance, won out in the end. As a concession to nearly half of the framers of the U.S. Constitution who favored the Paterson Plan over the Randolph Plan, the U.S. Senate was created. During just two centuries it came to be one of the world's most powerful legislative bodies.

As for William Paterson, the fiery proponent of the rights of small states became an associate justice of the U.S. Supreme Court (in an era when the court had not yet gained its present vast prestige and power). Paterson died in 1806, decades too early to know that eventually the U.S. legislative system would yield a double bonus to the state he so fervently represented in 1787.

Today, geographically tiny New Jersey is on equal footing in the U.S. Senate with vast states like Texas and California. At the same time, growth of urban population has given New Jersey more than ordinary clout in the House of Representatives. Alaska, Delaware,

Hawaii, Idaho, Maine, Nevada, North Dakota, Rhode Island, Utah, and Wyoming, *combined,* have one less voice in the House than does New Jersey with her fifteen representatives.

Ardent Jerseyman that he was, even William Paterson wouldn't have had the nerve to demand for his state such a role as it has been given by the unique U.S. mix of House-plus-Senate that makes up the Congress.

Battling Malaria and Other Fevers, John Gorrie, M.D., Accidentally Stumbled on the Mechanical Refrigerator

In the era before the Civil War, Apalachicola, Florida, flourished as the third largest cotton market on the Gulf Coast. At least two dozen steamers were in continuous use on the Chattahoochee, Apalachicola, and Flint rivers—bringing the cotton of western Georgia and eastern Alabama to the port. Because much cotton was purchased by agents for European firms, the city was cosmopolitan to a degree not suggested by its present rank among U.S. metropolitan centers.

John Gorrie, M.D., came to Apalachicola in 1833 because the thriving city offered a good opportunity for professional and business men. Scanty records of his early years indicate that he was born in Charleston, South Carolina, in 1803 and was educated in New York.

Malaria was the nearly-universal malady of the region. Most persons—including the majority of physicians—clung to the theory according to which it is an airborne disease. Quinine had been in use for decades, but especially during the long, hot summers patients "down with fever" were dreadfully uncomfortable.

Without any experimental evidence to back the idea, Gorrie became convinced that reduction of room temperature would affect the progress of malaria. To test that hunch he rigged up a primitive cooling system. Since he had no mechanical training or experience, it was far less elaborate than that later installed in the White House in a futile attempt to save the life of James A. Garfield.

Writing under the pen name "Jenner," the young physician described his apparatus in the Apalachicola *Commercial Advertiser* on May 18, 1844:

"The mechanical contrivance by which I propose to take advantage of these (cooling) properties of ice, so as to effect a refrigerating and depurating ventilation, is simple. My whole process consists of first suspending an ornamental vase, urn or basin, in which the ice is placed, by chains like a lamp or chandelier, from the center of and close to the ceiling of the room (in which fever-racked patients were kept).

"Next, over this vessel an opening is made in the ceiling from which a pipe is extended between the ceiling and the floor above, to the ceiling of the house" in order to produce air currents. Ice used in this system was cut from lakes and ponds of New England during winter, shipped south by steamer. During seasons of cold weather it sold for as little as five cents a pound—but by August it was likely to bring at least ten times as much. In years when the "ice crop" was poor, the precious stuff soared to $1.50 a pound when it reached New Orleans, Mobile, Apalachicola, Savannah, and other southern ports late in the summer.

Gorrie had studied just enough physics to know that when air that has been condensed is allowed to expand, it absorbs heat. So on May 25, 1844, another of his newspaper articles under the "Jenner" pen name told readers that:

"It is proposed to compress the external atmosphere by means of a force pump, and transfer it into a reservoir, and thence transmit it to a similar pump, there to exert its expanding mechanical force, and, finally, be discharged into the room of a house, or in the cabin, or under the deck of a vessel . . . to obtain large quantities of the 'principal of cold' at a comparatively smaller cost than by any other known method."

Essentially, then, the physician expected to employ two force pumps for condensation and expansion of air, with a storage chamber between pumps for dissipation of heat. His goal was a reliable and inexpensive supply of cool air for use with his patients fighting fever plus natural heat. Two rooms in Gorrie's home were converted to "hospital" use and the apparatus was placed in operation—probably but not positively during the summer of 1844.

During the following year the air-pumps were running at full speed, powered by a steam engine. Someone—either nurse Betsey Liverman or Gorrie's houseman—forgot to turn off the steam engines when temperatures began to drop at night. Next morning, pipes that handled the flow of outgoing air were found clogged with ice.

That accident on a summer night in 1845 convinced the physician that it would be possible to manufacture ice by means of machinery. He experimented for five years, developed a metal container about the size of a building block (or brick). When properly positioned, the container became a freezing unit that produced a brick-size cake of ice "as hard as that formed by nature."

Gorrie, strangely, found it easier to make ice than to remove it from the freezing unit. He tried greasing the container, even experimented with a churn-shaped cylinder with the hope that ice would slip readily from it. It didn't. Still the physician turned inventor continued his experiments.

He went to New Orleans to find capital to finance the building of model icemaking machines in a Cincinnati iron works. These went, respectively, to London and to Washington—along with applications for patents. London responded more promptly than did Washington; British patent #13,234 was granted on August 22, 1850. U.S. patent #8080 was not issued until May 6, 1851.

Long before he had full legal control of his invention, Gorrie had given a public demonstration at Mansion House, a noted hotel in the city where ice was first made by mechanical means. Guests at the dinner were awed—but the general public cared little for the fact that man had reached another milestone in his ceaseless struggle to control his environment. Especially in New England and in New York, newspapers ridiculed the idea of man-made ice. It couldn't possibly be the same as ice made by God (and besides, it threatened the region's important ice-cutting and storing industry).

A full-size icemaking machine, also manufactured in Cincinnati, brought the inventor some offers from investors—but not enough to warrant placing it on the market. He died in June, 1855, just five years after giving that dramatic demonstration in Mansion House hotel, Apalachicola. Deeply disappointed and a bit bitter that his machine had failed to win acclaim, he didn't know that his model would eventually be displayed in the Smithsonian Institute as tangible evidence supporting his claim to fame as "the father of refrigeration."

Index